Introduction to Daily Language Review

Why *Daily Language Review*?

The premise behind *Daily Language Review* is simple and straightforward—frequent, focused practice leads to mastery and retention of the skills practiced.

What's in *Daily Language Review*?

The book is divided into 36 weekly sections. There are five practice items for each day of the week.

Monday through Thursday follow this format:

- two sentences to edit—corrections need to be made in punctuation, capitalization, and grammar.

- three items that practice a variety of language and reading skills.

Friday's practice cycles through four different formats:

- *identifying mistakes*—deciding if marked sections of a reading passage contain punctuation, capitalization, and spelling errors.

- *combining sentences*—combining two simple sentences to form one more sophisticated sentence.

- *language usage practice*—choosing correct verb form, pronoun, homophone, etc., to use in a sentence.

- *reference materials*—choosing whether to use an encyclopedia, almanac, dictionary, thesaurus, or phone book to find information.

An Answer Key for each week is provided on the same page as the Friday lesson.

Scope and sequence charts on pages 3 and 4 detail the specific skills practiced and show in which weeks the practice occurs. The skills included are those found in language texts at this level.

How to Use *Daily Language Review*

There are several ways that the daily review practices can be presented. You may want to use all of these presentations throughout the year to help keep the practice fresh and interesting.

1. Make overhead transparencies of the lessons. Conduct the practice as an oral activity with the entire class. Write answers and make corrections using an erasable pen.

   Increased retention of the skills will occur if students mark the answers at the same time on a reproduced sheet or write the answers on writing paper. As the class becomes more familiar with *Daily Language Review*, you may want students to mark their own answers first and then check responses by marking the items on the transparency.

2. Reproduce the pages for individuals or partners to work independently. Check answers as a group using an overhead transparency to model the correct answers.

   Use these pages as independent practice only after much oral group experience with the lessons.

3. Occasionally you may want to use a day's, or even a week's, lesson as a test to see how individuals are progressing in their acquisition of skills.

It should be stressed, however, that the greatest learning benefit will be gained from doing the practices orally so that students continually hear correct responses modeled by their classmates and the teacher.

Hints, Suggestions, and Options

1. Look ahead several weeks at the skills being practiced. If possible, teach new skills in formal lessons before asking students to practice these skills in the daily review.

2. Sometimes you will not have taught a given skill before it appears in a lesson. These items should then be done together. Tell the class that there is a skill they have not yet been taught. See if anyone knows the answer and wishes to explain it to the class. If not, use the review time to conduct a mini-lesson on that skill.

3. Customize the daily review lessons to the needs of your class.

   • If there are skills that are not included in the grade level expectancies of the particular program you teach, you may choose to skip those items—white them out or correct them before reproducing the page.

   • If you feel your class needs more practice than is provided, add these "extras" on your own. For example:

      Use the daily "edit" sentences to locate subject, predicate, parts of speech, etc.

      Add a one-item warm up, a mini-post test, or ask students to provide another example.

Skills Scope and Sequence

Punctuation & Grammar: Abbreviations · Language Usage · Parts of Speech · Possessive Nouns · Sentence Structure · Sentence Types · Singular/Plural Nouns · Subject/Predicate · Verb Tense

Comprehension: Analogies · Categorizing · Cause & Effect · Fact/Fantasy · Fact/Opinion · Fiction/Nonfiction · Setting/Inference

Vocabulary/Word Study: Base Word/Prefix/Suffix · Contractions · Homophones · Rhyme · Synonyms/Antonyms · Vowel Sounds · Word Meaning from Context

Reference Skills: Alphabetical Order · Dictionary Guide Words · Reference Materials · Syllabication

Other Language Skills: Correct/Incorrect Spelling · Friendly Letter · Identify the Mistake · Sentence Combination

Week	Abbreviations	Language Usage	Parts of Speech	Possessive Nouns	Sentence Structure	Sentence Types	Singular/Plural Nouns	Subject/Predicate	Verb Tense
Week 1								X	
Week 2								X	
Week 3								X	
Week 4	X								
Week 5		X			X				
Week 6									X
Week 7		X					X		
Week 8		X		X		X	X		
Week 9		X					X	X	
Week 10			X	X					
Week 11							X		
Week 12				X					
Week 13									
Week 14					X				
Week 15		X	X				X		
Week 16							X		
Week 17							X		
Week 18		X		X					
Week 19			X	X				X	
Week 20							X	X	
Week 21	X	X		X					
Week 22							X		
Week 23	X			X					
Week 24	X			X			X		
Week 25				X					
Week 26		X			X	X			
Week 27		X			X	X			
Week 28			X						
Week 29									
Week 30							X		
Week 31	X		X		X				
Week 32	X	X	X	X					
Week 33	X		X	X					
Week 34	X								
Week 35				X					
Week 36	X								

Sentence Editing Skills

This scope-and-sequence chart tracks skills covered in Weeks 1–36. Column groups (as labeled): **Grammar & Usage** (Correct Article/Determiner/, Adjective, Double Negatives, Pronouns, Homophones, Verb Forms); **Apostrophe** (Contractions, Possessives); **Comma** (Words in a Series; Dates, Addresses; to Separate Dialogue); **Quotation Marks** (in Speech; Songs, Poems, Short Stories); **Punctuation** (End of Sentence, Period Abbreviations, Colon in Time, Underline Books/Magazine/Plays, Run-on Sentences); **Capitalization** (Beginning of Sentence; Books, Songs, Poems, Titles; of People; Other Proper Nouns).

	Grammar & Usage						Apostrophe		Comma			Quotation Marks		Punctuation					Capitalization			
Week	Verb Forms	Homophones	Pronouns	Double Neg.	Adjective	Correct Article	Possessives	Contractions	Separate Dialogue	Dates, Addr.	Words in Series	Songs/Poems/Stories	in Speech	Run-on Sent.	Underline Books	Colon in Time	Period Abbr.	End of Sentence	Other Proper Nouns	of People	Books/Songs/Titles	Beginning of Sentence
Week 1	✗		✗								✗			✗			✗		✗			✗
Week 2	✗	✗	✗								✗			✗			✗		✗	✗		✗
Week 3	✗	✗						✗			✗	✗	✗	✗			✗		✗	✗		✗
Week 4	✗	✗	✗					✗			✗			✗			✗		✗	✗		✗
Week 5	✗	✗		✗				✗			✗	✗		✗					✗	✗		✗
Week 6	✗		✗								✗			✗			✗					✗
Week 7	✗			✗				✗			✗			✗			✗		✗			✗
Week 8	✗	✗	✗				✗	✗						✗			✗		✗	✗		✗
Week 9	✗	✗	✗								✗		✗	✗					✗			✗
Week 10	✗	✗	✗		✗		✗				✗			✗	✗		✗		✗	✗		✗
Week 11	✗								✗	✗				✗	✗							✗
Week 12	✗			✗	✗			✗						✗			✗		✗			✗
Week 13	✗	✗	✗		✗			✗			✗	✗		✗								✗
Week 14	✗													✗								✗
Week 15	✗	✗	✗		✗		✗	✗			✗	✗		✗	✗				✗	✗		✗
Week 16	✗													✗	✗		✗					✗
Week 17	✗	✗	✗					✗			✗			✗								✗
Week 18	✗			✗										✗	✗	✗	✗		✗	✗		✗
Week 19	✗	✗	✗	✗				✗			✗			✗								✗
Week 20	✗	✗								✗	✗		✗	✗		✗			✗			✗
Week 21	✗		✗	✗						✗	✗		✗	✗					✗			✗
Week 22	✗		✗		✗		✗			✗	✗		✗	✗	✗				✗	✗		✗
Week 23	✗			✗					✗			✗	✗	✗			✗					✗
Week 24	✗	✗	✗	✗				✗		✗				✗			✗					✗
Week 25	✗	✗		✗				✗					✗	✗					✗			✗
Week 26	✗	✗	✗					✗	✗	✗			✗	✗	✗				✗			✗
Week 27	✗	✗	✗	✗				✗			✗		✗	✗					✗			✗
Week 28	✗	✗												✗								✗
Week 29	✗	✗	✗		✗			✗	✗					✗	✗	✗			✗	✗		✗
Week 30	✗										✗		✗	✗					✗			✗
Week 31	✗	✗	✗						✗		✗	✗		✗					✗			✗
Week 32	✗	✗		✗							✗	✗	✗	✗					✗	✗		✗
Week 33	✗	✗	✗	✗				✗	✗				✗	✗	✗				✗			✗
Week 34	✗	✗					✗						✗	✗					✗			✗
Week 35	✗	✗		✗			✗						✗	✗								✗
Week 36	✗	✗			✗						✗		✗	✗					✗			✗

Monday 1

Correct these sentences.

1. did you hear mother calling you to dinner

2. the meeting starts at 915

Which word IS spelled correctly?

3. doess   duz   does   doose

Fact or opinion?

4. Superman wears a blue suit and a red cape.

5. The grass is too long.

Tuesday 1

Which word IS spelled correctly?

1. tooda   toda   today   todey

2. bowl   bowle   boal   boole

Correct these sentences.

3. me and marcos will ride the bus together

4. him don't know anyone named james

Use context clues to determine the meaning of the bolded word below.

5. The door was **ajar**, and we felt a breeze from outside.

Name: _____

Wednesday ⬠1

Correct these sentences.

1. she bought apples carrots and cereal

_____

2. mary she is going to be late for the lesson

_____

Complete this analogy.

3. fire : hot :: ice : _____

Which word IS spelled correctly?

4. frend   freind   friend   frund

5. hapiness   happiness   happeness   happines

Name: _____

Thursday ⬠1

Which word IS spelled correctly?

1. wanted   whanted   waunted   want'd

Correct these sentences.

2. my dad taked my sisters bike to be fixed

_____

3. he knowed what his homework was

_____

Where does each quotation probably take place?

4. "Julia, may I borrow your eraser?"   _____

5. "Swimmers take your mark, set, GO!"   _____

Read the following paragraph and decide if the underlined part has a capitalization error, punctuation error, spelling error, or no mistake. Fill in the circle beside the answer you choose.

Owls <u>are interesting birds?</u> They all <u>have feathers, bones</u> that are hollow,
   1   2

<u>and lay egs. Owls eat mice</u> and other <u>rodents They eat</u> the entire animal and
   3   4

then cough up a small pellet <u>of the rodents bones.</u>
                                  5

1. ○ capitalization   ○ punctuation   ○ spelling   ○ no mistake
2. ○ capitalization   ○ punctuation   ○ spelling   ○ no mistake
3. ○ capitalization   ○ punctuation   ○ spelling   ○ no mistake
4. ○ capitalization   ○ punctuation   ○ spelling   ○ no mistake
5. ○ capitalization   ○ punctuation   ○ spelling   ○ no mistake

---

Daily Language Review

Answer Key ⬠①

Monday
1. Did you hear mother calling you to dinner?
2. The meeting starts at 9:15.
3. does
4. fact
5. opinion

Tuesday
1. today
2. bowl
3. Marcos and I will ride the bus together.
4. He doesn't know anyone named James.
5. open slightly

Wednesday
1. She bought apples, carrots, and cereal.
2. Mary (or She) is going to be late for the lesson.
3. fire : hot :: ice : cold
4. friend
5. happiness

Thursday
1. wanted
2. My dad took my sister's bike to be fixed.
3. He knew what his homework was.
4. school
5. swimming pool

Friday
1. punctuation
2. no mistake
3. spelling
4 punctuation
5. punctuation

Name: _____

Monday 2

Correct these sentences.

1. does you have a dog or a cat

_____

2. me and william like to help mr smith wash the chalkboards

_____

Give two words that rhyme with the following word.

3. ring _____

Which word IS spelled correctly?

4. neer   near   neare   kneer

5. seet   sete   cete   seat

Name: _____

Tuesday 2

Complete these analogies.

1. elephant : enormous :: mouse : _____

2. no corners : round :: 4 corners : _____

Use context clues to determine the meaning of the bolded word below.

3. The cars waited for the **pedestrian** to walk across the street.

_____

Correct these sentences.

4. have you read a book called the day jimmy's boa ate the wash

_____

5. i and chris will not be in the same class this year

Use context clues to determine the meaning of the bolded word below.

1. He had never ridden a horse before and was a **novice**.

_____

Correct these sentences.

2. are you going to charlotte north carolina this june

_____

3. we are reading a book called skinnybones by barbara park

_____

_____

Which word IS spelled correctly?

4. inneresting   interesing   interesting   intresting

5. suppose   supose   sappose   sapos

Complete these analogies.

1. eighteen : even :: thirty-three : _____

2. Chicago Bulls : basketball :: _____ : _____

Fact or fantasy?

3. The fairy flew in through the window. _____

Correct these sentences.

4. mr and mrs hill got a new baby named taylor

_____

5. in music class we singed to songs

_____

Name:

Friday ⬠2

Read the following paragraph and decide if the underlined part has a capitalization error, punctuation error, spelling error, or no mistake. Fill in the circle beside the answer you choose.

A <u>lobster is A water animal</u> with a <u>harrd shell that lives</u> on the bottom of the
       1   **2**

ocean <u>near the shore?</u> Lobsters have no <u>backbone. they</u> belong to a group
      3   **4**

<u>of animals called</u> crustaceans.
    5

1. ⭕ capitalization   ⭕ punctuation   ⭕ spelling   ⭕ no mistake
2. ⭕ capitalization   ⭕ punctuation   ⭕ spelling   ⭕ no mistake
3. ⭕ capitalization   ⭕ punctuation   ⭕ spelling   ⭕ no mistake
4. ⭕ capitalization   ⭕ punctuation   ⭕ spelling   ⭕ no mistake
5. ⭕ capitalization   ⭕ punctuation   ⭕ spelling   ⭕ no mistake

Answer Key ⬠2

Monday
1. Do you have a dog or a cat?
2. William and I like to help Mr. Smith wash the chalkboards.
3. Answers will vary.
4. near
5. seat

Tuesday
1. small or tiny
2. square or rectangle
3. someone who walks
4. Have you read a book called <u>The Day Jimmy's Boa Ate the Wash</u>?
5. Chris and I will not be in the same class this year.

Wednesday
1. beginner
2. Are you going to Charlotte, North Carolina, this June?
3. We are reading a book called <u>Skinnybones</u> by Barbara Park.
4. interesting
5. suppose

Thursday
1. odd
2. Answers will vary (team name: sport).
3. fantasy
4. Mr. and Mrs. Hill have a new baby named Taylor.
5. In music class we sang two songs.

Friday
1. capitalization
2. spelling
3. punctuation
4. capitalization
5. no mistake

              Daily Language Review Grade 3 EMC 581

Monday 3

Which word IS spelled correctly?

1. mose   mowse   mowce   mouse

Complete these analogies.

2. square : four :: triangle : _____

3. soccer ball : black and white :: basketball : _____

Correct these sentences.

4. there family has went to the yellowstone national park

_____

5. his homework it is in his backpack

_____

Tuesday 3

Correct these sentences.

1. dr stevens lives at 3434 old forge lane

_____

2. dont forget to turn the stove off after cooking

_____

Which word is NOT spelled correctly?

3. douwt   adjust   party   collar

4. juggle   iland   present   fault

Fact or opinion?

5. Cats are the nicest pets to have. _____

Wednesday 3

Complete these analogies.

1. Sept. : September :: Nov. : ....

2. Mississippi : river :: Atlantic : ....

Correct these sentences.

3. gabriel said i returned the library book last tuesday

....

4. we listened to the song cherish on the radio

....

Use context clues to determine the meaning of the bolded word below.

5. He hadn't had lunch and was **famished** by dinner time.

....

Thursday 3

Correct these sentences.

1. he dont want seconds of the tuna salad

....

2. the flight attendant said put your tray tables upright and fasten your seatbelts

....

....

Which word is NOT spelled correctly?

3. today   noise   grumpie   seat

Give an antonym for each word.

4. hot ....

5. even ....

Name:

Friday ⬠3

Read the following paragraph and decide if the underlined part has a capitalization error, punctuation error, spelling error, or no mistake. Fill in the circle beside the answer you choose.

The term "cat" includes wild animals such as <u>tigers lions,</u> leopards, and
1

panthers as well as <u>the house cat? Cats have a</u> good <u>sense of balance</u> and
2 **3**

<u>can walk easily Along the</u> tops of <u>narrow spaces and allong narrow</u> ledges.
4 **5**

1. ○ capitalization　　○ punctuation　　○ spelling　　○ no mistake
2. ○ capitalization　　○ punctuation　　○ spelling　　○ no mistake
3. ○ capitalization　　○ punctuation　　○ spelling　　○ no mistake
4. ○ capitalization　　○ punctuation　　○ spelling　　○ no mistake
5. ○ capitalization　　○ punctuation　　○ spelling　　○ no mistake

Answer Key ⬠3

Monday
1. mouse
2. three
3. black and orange
4. Their family has gone to Yellowstone National Park.
5. His homework is in his backpack.

Tuesday
1. Dr. Stevens lives at 3434 Old Forge Lane.
2. Don't forget to turn the stove off after cooking.
3. douwt (doubt)
4. iland (island)
5. opinion

Wednesday
1. November
2. ocean
3. Gabriel said, "I returned the library book last Tuesday."
4. We listened to the song "Cherish" on the radio.
5. hungry, starving

Thursday
1. He doesn't want seconds of the tuna salad.
2. The flight attendant said, "Put your tray tables upright and fasten your seatbelts."
3. grumpie (grumpy)
4. cold, freezing
5. odd, uneven

Friday
1. punctuation
2. punctuation
3. no mistake
4. capitalization
5. spelling

　　　　13

Monday ⬠4

Complete these analogies.

1. picture : see :: music : _____

2. cat : meow :: pig : _____

Correct these sentences.

3. him and me are going to the library to check out the book the boxcar children

_____

_____

4. christmas is my favorite holiday

_____

Use context clues to determine the meaning of the bolded word below.

5. After borrowing money from her friend, she was **indebted** to her for $2.

Tuesday ⬠4

Correct these sentences.

1. the show that you wants to watch is on today it begins at 430

_____

_____

2. mr davis, the butcher, cut turkey ham and cheese for us

_____

_____

Give a synonym for the word below.

3. enormous _____

Which word is NOT spelled correctly?

4. married   bicycle   bilding   enemies

5. away   voiced   dinosaur   skrub

Wednesday ⬠4

Use context clues to determine the meaning of the bolded words below.

1. We could not see the sun because it was **overcast**. ....

2. The noisy kids were told to **vacate** the movie theatre. ....

Complete this analogy.

3. addition : + :: subtraction : ....

Correct these sentences.

4. dr rhodes said that my stomachache was from eating to many candy bars

....

....

5. watch out for that bus

....

Thursday ⬠4

Past, present, or future?

1. My dog Butch is running to catch a squirrel. ....

2. Dad flew to New York for business. ....

Correct these sentences.

3. i dont understand how he done the math problem

....

4. this april ms henning, my teacher, will gets married

....

Which word is NOT spelled correctly?

5. duz   laugh   system   mammal

Name:

Friday ④

Combine the two sentences to make one sentence.

1. Joan Schultze is a doctor. She lives in Oregon.

2. Our dog is seven years old. Her name is Molly.

3. My uncle is coming to visit us. He will be here Tuesday.

4. Cinderella swept the steps. Cinderella washed the floor.

5. I am scared of mice. I am scared of spiders too.

Answer Key ④

Monday
1. hear
2. oink, snort
3. He and I are going to the library to check out the book The Boxcar Children.
4. Christmas is my favorite holiday.
5. owed

Tuesday
1. The show that you want to watch is on today. It begins at 4:30.
2. Mr. Davis, the butcher, cut turkey, ham, and cheese for us.
3. huge, large, tremendous
4. bilding (building)
5. skrub (scrub)

Wednesday
1. cloudy
2. leave
3. - (subtraction sign)
4. Dr. Rhodes said that my stomachache was from eating too many candy bars.
5. Watch out for that bus!

Thursday
1. present
2. past
3. I don't understand how he did the math problem.
4. This April Ms. Henning, my teacher, will get married.
5. duz (does)

Friday
Sentences will vary somewhat. Accept any reasonable sentence construction that contains all the information.
1. Joan Schultze is a doctor who lives in Oregon.
2. Our dog Molly is seven years old.
3. My uncle is coming to visit us on Tuesday.
4. Cinderella swept the steps and washed the floor.
5. I am scared of mice and spiders.

Monday ⬠5

What is the correct way to divide each word into syllables?

1. p-encil   pen-cil   penc-il

2. play-ground   playgr-ound   pla-yground

Which words are plural nouns?

3. dancing   dishes   danced   slippers   slipped

Correct these sentences.

4. what color is your car asked samuel

_____

5. he aint gonna want no cookies cake or ice cream for dessert

_____

_____

Tuesday ⬠5

Give an antonym for the word below.

1. cheerful _____

Which word IS spelled correctly?

2. are   ar   arr

3. wher   where   werre

Correct these sentences.

4. for her sixth birthday she wanted a party at chuck e cheeses

_____

_____

5. the hours of the store was from 900 until 600

Wednesday ⑤

Correct these sentences.

1. on thursday night their will be a lunar eclipse

2. last saturday i left my glove at the ball field

Which word is NOT spelled correctly?

3. cheef   again   half   product

A, B, C, or D?

4. Mom said I _____ go.

   A. couldn't   B. couldnt   C. could'nt   D. Couldn't

5. The teacher moved all of the _____ desks.

   A. studen'ts   B. students   C. student's   D. students'

Thursday ⑤

Complete the analogies.

1. pair : two :: dozen : _____

2. 5 : nickel :: 10 : _____

Use context clues to determine the meaning of the bolded word below.

3. Rex is a **feisty** dog and is always ready to fight.

Correct these sentences.

4. the pilot will landed the plane in kalamazoo michigan

5. oscar cant get the present to him until next sunday

Name:

Friday 5

Combine the two sentences to make one sentence.

1. He wants a baseball glove. He needs it for the game.

_____

2. Jerrod has three sisters. Jerrod is the youngest.

_____

3. We took a walk around the block. We walked an hour.

_____

4. Do you know the time? Do you wear a watch?

_____

5. The ornaments were pretty. There were many of them.

_____

Daily Language Review

Answer Key 5

Monday
1. pen-cil
2. play-ground
3. dishes, slippers
4. "What color is your car?" asked Samuel.
5. He isn't going to want any cookies, cake, or ice cream for dessert.

Tuesday
1. sad, unhappy
2. are
3. where
4. For her sixth birthday she wanted a party at Chuck E. Cheese's.
5. The hours of the store were from 9:00 until 6:00.

Wednesday
1. On Thursday night there will be a lunar eclipse.
2. Last Saturday I left my glove at the ball field.
3. cheef (chief)
4. A. couldn't
5. D. students'

Thursday
1. twelve
2. dime
3. scrappy, ready to take action
4. The pilot will land the plane in Kalamazoo, Michigan.
5. Oscar can't get the present to him until next Sunday.

Friday
Sentences will vary. Accept any reasonable sentence that contains all the information.
1. He wants a baseball glove for the game.
2. Jerrod has three older sisters.
3. We took an hour walk around the block.
4. Do you wear a watch and know the time?
5. The many ornaments were pretty.

Name:

Monday 6

Correct these sentences.

1. this weekend him and i went to the san diego zoo

_____

2. my mother and father has been married since june 14 1968

_____

_____

A, B, C, or D?

3. The correct abbreviation for the word Sunday is:

   A. Sun.   B. Sun   C. Sun: D. Sund.

4. The "ei" in reindeer sounds most like the vowel sound in

   A. let   B. term   C. age   D. ice

What is the root or base word?

5. friendly _____

Name:

Tuesday 6

Give a synonym for each word below.

1. smart _____

2. said _____

Correct these sentences.

3. in august we will have a surprise 30th birthday party for aron

_____

_____

4. jane morris will be 29 on august 1 1997

_____

_____

Use context clues to determine the meaning of the bolded word below.

5. Hanna didn't know where the Indian Ocean was, so she looked in an **atlas**.

Name:

Wednesday 6

Correct these sentences.

1. have you ever traveled on a boat bus or train

_____

2. he wants to go to seattle washington in october

_____

What is the correct way to divide each word into syllables?

3. su-mmer   summ-er   sum-mer

4. fis-hing   fish-ing   fi-shing

Which word is NOT spelled correctly?

5. knew   glue   school   spred

Name:

Thursday 6

Correct these sentences.

1. dr ellis has brung the prescription to his patient

_____

2. austin is the capital of the state of texas

_____

Past, present, or future?

3. She went to the pool to find her mom. _____

4. He will get the book for his birthday. _____

Give an opinion about this topic.

5. McDonald's french fries

Friday

Combine the two sentences to make one sentence.

1. We are going to Sam's house. We will leave at 4:30.

_____

2. Sara knows her addition facts. She knows her subtraction facts too.

_____

3. Jason is five years old. Henry is six years old.

_____

4. I will order pepperoni pizza. I'll order a salad first.

_____

5. Our family has two girls and a boy. The boy's name is Stephen.

_____

Daily Language Review

Answer Key 6

Monday
1. This weekend he and I went to the San Diego Zoo.
2. My mother and father have been married since June 14, 1968.
3. A. Sun.
4. C. age
5. friend

Tuesday
1. intelligent, brainy, bright...
2. stated, explained, retorted...
3. In August we will have a surprise 30th birthday party for Aron.
4. Jane Morris will be 29 on August 1, 1997.
5. book of maps

Wednesday
1. Have you ever traveled on a boat, bus, or train?
2. He wants to go to Seattle, Washington, in October.
3. sum-mer
4. fish-ing
5. spred (spread)

Thursday
1. Dr. Ellis has brought the prescription to his patient.
2. Austin is the capital of the state of Texas.
3. past
4. future
5. Answers will vary.

Friday
Sentences will vary. Accept any reasonable sentence construction that contains all the information.
1. We are going to Sam's house at 4:30.
2. Sara knows her addition and subtraction facts.
3. Jason is five and Henry is six years old.
4. I'll order a salad first and then pepperoni pizza.
5. Our family has two girls and a boy named Stephen.

Monday ⑦

Use context clues to determine the meaning of the bolded words below.

1. Don't forget to put quotation marks around **dialogue**.

_____

2. His brother bothered him all afternoon and made him **irate**.

_____

Correct these sentences.

3. the plane is gonna be late it wont arrive until 1206

_____

4. jose aint got no pencils sharpened

_____

Which words have 3 syllables?

5. playground   enormous   predicate   recycle

                 ⬠   ⬠   ⬠

Tuesday ⑦

Correct these sentences.

1. on tuesday we will see a play called cinderella

_____

2. mrs jinkins, the librarian, will meets with the class at 830 am

_____

_____

Which word is NOT spelled correctly?

3. grocery   dropping   future   skream

4. pensil   quick   dolphin   arms

Where does the following event probably take place?

5. Lupe put the milk back in the refrigerator. _____

Name: _____

Wednesday ⑦

Correct these sentences.

1. tom dillion had for dimes two nickels and seven pennies

_____

2. dont forget to pick up the dry cleaning mother said

_____

Which word is NOT spelled correctly?

3. slim   catcher   whindow   zipper

4. ornge   afraid   pizza   knee

Complete this analogy.

5. car : steering wheel :: bike : _____

Name: _____

Thursday ⑦

Give an antonym for the words below.

1. interesting _____

2. finish _____

Correct these sentences.

3. what time do the movie start

_____

4. my dog baily digs up the flowers plants and grass

_____

Use this homophone pair in one sentence.

5. sea, see

Choose the word that best completes each sentence.

1. I will _____ the sidewalk to the pool.

    followed   follow   follow   following

2. Joe and _____ have been friends since kindergarten.

    me   us   I   we

3. Do you _____ how to write in cursive?

    know   knows   now   knew

4. Mrs. Payne, our principal, _____ us the school song.

    learned   learn   taught   teached

5. I _____ lived in Ann Arbor, Michigan, for three years.

    has   have   been   be

Monday
1. conversation, talking, exact words
2. angry, mad
3. The plane is going to be late. It won't arrive until 12:06.
4. Jose doesn't have any pencils sharpened.
5. enormous, predicate, recycle

Tuesday
1. On Tuesday we will see a play called Cinderella.
2. Mrs. Jinkins, the librarian, will meet with the class at 8:30 a.m.
3. skream (scream)
4. pensil (pencil)
5. kitchen

Wednesday
1. Tom Dillion had four dimes, two nickels, and seven pennies.
2. "Don't forget to pick up the dry cleaning," mother said.
3. whindow (window)
4. ornge (orange)
5. handlebars

Thursday
1. dull, boring
2. start, begin
3. What time does the movie start?
4. My dog Baily digs up the flowers, plants, and grass.
5. Answers will vary.

Friday
1. follow
2. I
3. know
4. taught
5. have

Name: _____

Monday 8

Correct these sentences.

1. dontcha have anything to trade for lunch

_____

2. he wants to know if you is going on the field trip

_____

Fact or opinion?

3. Going to the beach is the best vacation. _____

4. Mars is called the "red planet."

Common or proper noun?

5. Coca Cola _____

Name: _____

Tuesday 8

Which word is NOT spelled correctly?

1. swimming   climbed   thick   wold

2. knock   boxes   cirkus   alphabet

Give a synonym for the following word.

3. afraid _____

Correct these sentences.

4. mrs pope, the music teacher, told us to bring a pencil to class

_____

_____

5. we hopes you have a happy halloween

_____

Wednesday 8

Correct these sentences.

1. harrys shirt is to small for his brother to borrow

2. the score of the baseball game was dolphins 0, hawks 7

Where do the following events probably take place?

3. Everyone is supposed to stay seated, face forward, and hold their backpacks on their laps.

4. Go down the slide one at a time.

Complete this analogy.

5. steak : dinner :: cereal :

Thursday 8

Which words have 2 syllables?

1. number   holler   rainbow   computer

Correct these sentences.

2. i told dr shirley about a great book called iggy's house

3. dominique has went to fill up her car with gas at the exxon station

Underline the correct, complete sentence.

4. The boy put on skates he ties the laces. The kite flew high in the sky.

5. The dog saw a cat, and it started barking. The dog ran away the boy chased it.

Friday 8

Choose the word that best completes each sentence.

1. Will you pass _____ the catsup?

   my   me   we   they

2. The play _____ at 7:15.

   begun   will begin   start   beginned

3. We _____ our grandmother a can opener.

   gots   buyed   gived   bought

4. Carol, my friend, _____ German very well.

   speak   speaks   speaked   spoked

5. When I was 13, I _____ to Italy with my Dad.

   went   goed   was going   had went

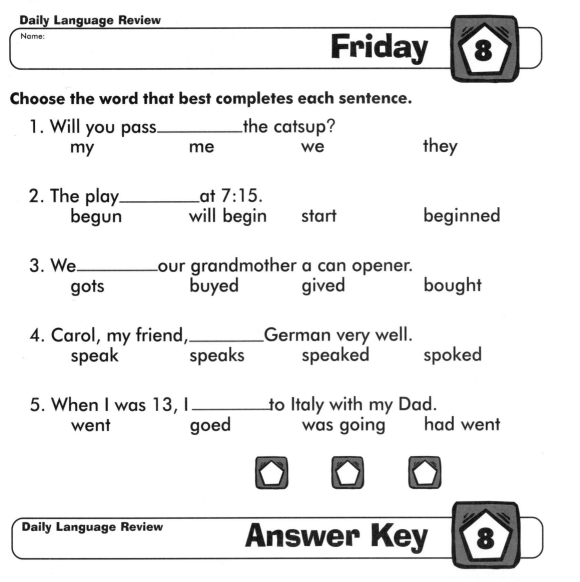

Daily Language Review

Answer Key 8

Monday _____
1. Don't you have anything to trade for lunch?
2. He wants to know if you are going on the field trip.
3. opinion
4. fact
5. proper noun

Tuesday _____
1. wold (would)
2. cirkus (circus)
3. scared, fearful, timid...
4. Mrs. Pope, the music teacher, told us to bring a pencil to class.
5. We hope you have a happy Halloween.

Wednesday _____
1. Harry's shirt is too small for his brother to borrow. 2. The score of the baseball game was Dolphins 0, Hawks 7.
3. school bus
4. playground, slide
5. breakfast

Thursday _____
1. number, holler, rainbow
2. I told Dr. Shirley about a great book called Iggy's House.
3. Dominique has gone to fill up her car with gas at the Exxon station.
4. The kite flew high in the sky.
5. The dog saw a cat, and it started barking.

Friday _____
1. me
2. will begin
3. bought
4. speaks
5. went

Name:

Monday ⑨

Which word comes first in alphabetical order?

1. flash   fence   false   fight

2. trade   tie   tape   tugboat

If the guide words on a page were <u>rain</u> and <u>road</u> which word would be on the page?

3. rent   rage   rope   run

Correct these sentences.

4. have you ever read time magazine

_____

5. we seen the x-ray the broken bone was in the hand

_____

Name:

Tuesday ⑨

Give an antonym for the following word.

1. light _____

Correct these sentences.

2. for dinner i would rather ate spaghetti than pizza

_____

3. he went fishing caught three fish and cooked them for dinner

_____

_____

Which word is NOT spelled correctly?

4. rough   sharck   since   balloon

5. afeter   morning   scare   summer

Wednesday ⑨

Correct these sentences.

1. we sang the song america, the beautiful in music class

_____

2. david has gave his soccer equipment to jason and i

_____

Which is the correct way to divide each word into syllables?

3. jumpi-ng   jum-ping   jump-ing

4. foot-ball   footba-ll   foo-tball

Which word IS spelled correctly?

5. rimote   remot   remote   remoke

⬠   ⬠   ⬠

Thursday ⑨

A, B, or C?

1. My aunt was married on _____ .

   A. March 14, 1995   B. March, 14, 1995   C. March 14 1995

2. In June my family will fly to _____ .

   A. Orlando: Florida   B. Orlando. Florida   C. Orlando, Florida

What is the verb in the following sentence?

3. Her bicycle turned the corner.

Correct these sentences.

4. in australia students wear uniforms two school

_____

5. north america includes canada the united states and mexico

_____

Friday

Choose the word that best completes each sentence.

1. We will have to wait and let them do _____ job.
   they're   their   there

2. Nathan and Tyler _____ the song beautifully.
   is singing   sang   singed

3. We _____ the car wreck from our window.
   saw   seed   is seeing

4. I _____ two friends named Sandy.
   gots   have   has

5. Will you go _____ the bank and cash the check?
   two   to   too

Answer Key 9

Monday
1. false
2. tape
3. rent
4. Have you ever read Time magazine?
5. We saw the x-ray. The broken bone was in the hand.

Tuesday
1. heavy or dark
2. For dinner I would rather eat spaghetti than pizza.
3. He went fishing, caught three fish, and cooked them for dinner.
4. sharck (shark)
5. afeter (after)

Wednesday
1. We sang the song "America, the Beautiful" in music class.
2. David gave his soccer equipment to Jason and me.
3. jump-ing
4. foot-ball
5. remote

Thursday
1. A. March 14, 1995
2. C. Orlando, Florida
3. turned
4. In Australia students wear uniforms to school.
5. North America includes Canada, the United States, and Mexico.

Friday
1. their
2. sang
3. saw
4. have
5. to

Name:

Monday (10)

Statement, command, question, or exclamation?

1. Did you fly or drive to California? ....

2. Get out your math book. ....

Correct these sentences.

3. amy asked who borrowed my eraser

_____

4. dallas, dans dog, has ate all of his food

_____

Singular or plural?

5. cracker ....

Name:

Tuesday (10)

Correct these sentences.

1. laura and rebekah brung water on they're hike

_____

2. lets ride our bikes to the lake it will take a hour

_____

Give a sentence with each homophone pair.

3. flower, flour ....

4. I, eye ....

Which part of a friendly letter? Heading, greeting, body, closing, or signature?

5. Your friend, ...

Wednesday 10

Complete this analogy.

1. red + yellow : orange :: blue + yellow : ....

Correct these sentences.

2. mr poppers pengins is my favorite book

....

3. robin and ted have went running for too miles

....

Synonyms or antonyms?

4. on, off ....

5. glad, happy ....

Thursday 10

Correct these sentences.

1. i go to fielder elementary school

....

2. are you cheering for the mustangs or the tigers at the football game

....

Which word is NOT spelled correctly?

3. afraid   dollar   rain   dicide

4. broom   famly   fire   oil

Give two words that rhyme with the word below.

5. time ....

Friday ⑩

Which reference source would you need to find the following information:
dictionary, telephone book, or encyclopedia?

1. what street the closest grocery store is on _____

2. the years that Mozart lived _____

3. how to pronounce the word "excerpt" _____

4. the phone number for Sid's Bagels _____

5. what part of speech the word "trample" is _____

Answer Key ⑩

Daily Language Review

Monday
1. question
2. command
3. Amy asked, "Who borrowed my eraser?"
4. Dallas, Dan's dog, has eaten all of his food.
5. singular

Tuesday
1. Laura and Rebekah brought water on their hike.
2. Let's ride our bikes to the lake. It will take an hour.
3. Answers will vary.
4. Answers will vary.
5. closing

Wednesday
1. green
2. Mr. Popper's Penguins is my favorite book.
3. Robin and Ted went running for two miles.
4. antonyms
5. synonyms

Thursday
1. I go to Fielder Elementary School.
2. Are you cheering for the Mustangs or the Tigers at the football game?
3. dicide (decide)
4. famly (family)
5. Answers will vary.

Friday
1. telephone book
2. encyclopedia
3. dictionary
4. telephone book
5. dictionary

Name: _____

Monday 11

Which word is NOT spelled correctly?

1. coler   first   kind   worry

2. write   teath   flies   burned

Past, present, or future?

3. The roller coaster climbed up the hill. _____

Correct these sentences.

4. our family will be in miami florida this christmas

_____

5. would you learn me to read sign language

Name: _____

Tuesday 11

Give two words that rhyme with the word below.

1. five _____

Correct these sentences.

2. yesterday we read a poem called sick by shel silverstein

_____

_____

3. april 27 1997 is the day our report is due

_____

Which word comes first in alphabetical order?

4. south   same   sly   sky

5. odd   otter   out   open

Name: _____

Wednesday ⬡11

Complete the analogies.

1. lemon : yellow :: lime : ‒‒‒‒‒‒‒‒‒‒‒‒‒‒‒‒‒‒‒‒‒‒‒‒

2. peach : fuzzy :: watermelon : ‒‒‒‒‒‒‒‒‒‒‒‒‒‒‒‒‒‒‒‒

Which words would be on the same page as the guide words <u>odor</u> and <u>organ</u>?

3. oats   owner   other   old

Correct these sentences.

4. dad will be home from his trip on thursday evening said mom

‒‒

5. the refrigerator door was not closed, and someone leaved the light on

‒‒

‒‒

Name: _____

Thursday ⬠11

Which part of a friendly letter? Heading, greeting, body, closing, or signature?

1. Dear Allison, ‒‒‒‒‒‒‒‒‒‒‒‒‒‒‒‒‒‒‒‒‒‒‒‒‒‒‒‒‒‒‒‒‒‒‒

2. 2119 Mason Road ‒‒‒‒‒‒‒‒‒‒‒‒‒‒‒‒‒‒‒‒‒‒‒‒‒‒‒‒‒‒‒‒

Correct these sentences.

3. the library has five copies of dear mr henshaw, a great book

‒‒

4. we read the talking eggs, a short story, in language class

‒‒

The oo in school sounds most like the vowel sound in:

5. out   long   open   rule

Name:

Friday 11

Which reference source would you need to find the following information: dictionary, telephone book, or encyclopedia?

1. what part of speech the word "dive" is _____

2. what kind of animal an okapi is _____

3. where to find more articles about reptiles _____

4. the area code of Sarasota, Florida _____

5. other animals related to the Komodo dragon _____

Answer Key 11

Monday
1. coler (color)
2. teath (teeth)
3. past
4. Our family will be in Miami, Florida, this Christmas.
5. Would you teach me to read sign language?

Tuesday
1. Answers will vary.
2. Yesterday we read a poem called "Sick" by Shel Silverstein.
3. April 27, 1997, is the day our report is due.
4. same
5. odd

Wednesday
1. green
2. smooth
3. old
4. "Dad will be home from his trip on Thursday evening," said mom.
5. The refrigerator door was not closed, and someone left the light on.

Thursday
1. greeting
2. heading
3. The library has five copies of <u>Dear Mr. Henshaw</u>, a great book.
4. We read "The Talking Eggs," a short story, in language class.
5. rule

Friday
1. dictionary
2. encyclopedia
3. encyclopedia
4. telephone book
5. encyclopedia

Name: _____

Monday 12

Correct these sentences.

1. this summer we is going to camp illahee in the Appalachian mountains

_____

_____

2. frank ann and robert are going to see the movie at 445

_____

Which words have 2 syllables?

3. lipstick   interested   alligator   forget

4. none   number   catcher   batter

Use context clues to determine the meaning of the bolded word below.

5. The hummingbird **hovered** above the flower. _____

Name: _____

Tuesday 12

Fact, or fantasy?

1. Her car has a flat tire. _____

2. The car sprouted wings and flew away. _____

Combine these two sentences into one sentence.

3. Hobie has a cat. The cat's name is Elvis.

_____

Correct these sentences.

4. please tell me your phone number i will call you tonight

_____

_____

5. mr thomas and mr smythe will visit the museum tomorrow

_____

Wednesday (12)

Which words rhyme with shoe?

1. glue   dove   do   overdue

Correct these sentences.

2. my favorite restaurant is burger king

_____

3. the country that we are studying in social studies is italy

_____

_____

Where does each event probably take place?

4. John threw the ball to second base.

5. She fastened her seat belt when she sat down. _____

Thursday (12)

Correct these sentences.

1. we aint never hiked down the grand canyon

_____

2. aunt martha sent us a gift for hanukkah

_____

The "u" in mule sounds most like the vowel sounds in:

3. pull   tool   tune   music

Command, statement, question, or exclamation?

4. Look out for that car! _____

5. Half of one dollar is fifty cents.

Friday

Which reference source would you need to find the following information: dictionary, telephone book, or encyclopedia?

1. a dentist near my neighborhood

2. the phone number for Pizza Hut

3. information for a report on the snowy owl

4. how to spell the word "mesmerizing"

5. information about the Grand Canyon

Daily Language Review

Answer Key 12

Monday
1. This summer we are going to Camp Illahee in the Applachian Mountains.
2. Frank, Ann, and Robert are going to see the movie at 4:45.
3. lipstick, forget
4. number, catcher, batter
5. flew in one place, stayed in the air

Tuesday
1. fact
2. fantasy
3. Hobie has a cat named Elvis.
4. Please tell me your phone number. I will call you tonight.
5. Mr. Thomas and Mr. Smythe will visit the museum tomorrow.

Wednesday
1. glue, do, overdue
2. My favorite restaurant is Burger King.
3. The country that we are studying in social studies is Italy.
4. baseball field
5. car, truck, airplane

Thursday
1. We have never hiked down the Grand Canyon.
2. Aunt Martha sent us a gift for Hanukkah.
3. tool, tune, music
4. exclamation
5. statement

Friday
1. telephone book
2. telephone book
3. encyclopedia
4. dictionary
5. encyclopedia

Monday ⑬

Correct these sentences.

1. would you like bread with your salad

_____

2. does you need help with changing the bicycle tire

_____

Singular or plural noun?

3. dolphin _____

4. children _____

Which word is NOT spelled correctly?

5. daisy egg loop lern

Tuesday ⑬

Which is the correct way to divide each word into syllables?

1. swi-mm-ing swim-ming swimm-ing

2. cam-el came-l ca-mel

Correct these sentences.

3. me and her moved into a apartment to save money

_____

4. how many words a minute can you type asked the secretary

_____

_____

Use context clues to determine the meaning of the bolded word below.

5. The bully tried to **antagonize** the smaller boy by taking the his hat and

holding it out of reach. _____

Name: _____

Wednesday 13

Give a synonym for each word.

1. argue _____

2. hit _____

Correct these sentences.

3. the cashier rang up carrots pickles and pineapple

_____

4. her dog is trained to do for tricks

_____

Fact or opinion?

5. The speed limit on this road is too slow. _____

Name: _____

Thursday 13

Past, present, or future?

1. They drove to the mountains to visit Cousin Ruby. _____

Which IS the correct spelling?

2. meshure   measure   meazure

3. kage   caje   cage

Correct these sentences.

4. dana asked who is in charge here

_____

5. henry couldnt remember the combination to his lock

_____

Name: _____

Friday ⬠13

Read the following paragraph and decide if the underlined part has a capitalization error, punctuation error, spelling error, or no mistake. Fill in the circle beside the answer you choose.

An <u>earthquake happens when</u> a break <u>in the earths outer</u> shell causes the ground
       1   **2**

to <u>shake and shift Earthquakes</u> are one of the most <u>Powerful events on earth</u>.
        3   **4**

During some small earthquakes, the shaking of the ground <u>may be know more</u>
                                            5

noticeable than the shaking caused by a train's passing.

1. ○ capitalization   ○ punctuation   ○ spelling   ○ no mistake
2. ○ capitalization   ○ punctuation   ○ spelling   ○ no mistake
3. ○ capitalization   ○ punctuation   ○ spelling   ○ no mistake
4. ○ capitalization   ○ punctuation   ○ spelling   ○ no mistake
5. ○ capitalization   ○ punctuation   ○ spelling   ○ no mistake

---

Answer Key ⬠13

Monday
1. Would you like bread with your salad?
2. Do you need help with changing the bicycle tire?
3. singular
4. plural
5. lern (learn)

Tuesday
1. swim-ming
2. cam-el
3. She and I moved into an apartment to save money.
4. "How many words a minute can you type?" asked the secretary.
5. annoy, bother, pester

Wednesday
1. fight, bicker, quarrel
2. punch, smack, strike, slug
3. The cashier rang up carrots, pickles, and pineapple.
4. Her dog is trained to do four tricks.
5. opinion

Thursday
1. past
2. measure
3. cage
4. Dana asked, "Who is in charge here?"
5. Henry couldn't remember the combination to his lock.

Friday
1. no mistake
2. punctuation
3. punctuation
4. capitalization
5. spelling

Name: _____

Monday  14

Correct these sentences.

1. red yellow and blue are primary colors

_____

2. it was time for dinner i set the table

_____

Which is the adjective in each sentence?

3. There was a gold ring in the window.

4. Joe has four sisters who live in Nebraska.

Complete this analogy.

5. interesting : dull :: open : _____

Name: _____

Tuesday 14

Synonyms or antonyms?

1. now, later _____

2. normal, unusual _____

Correct these sentences.

3. have you read the enormous crocodile, a book by roald dahl

_____

_____

4. i really like to listen to the radio while I jog

_____

Is the underlined word a noun, verb, or adjective?

5. Amelia Bedelia took the class to see her <u>house</u>. _____

Wednesday 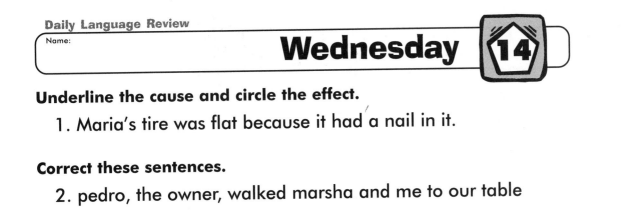 14

Underline the cause and circle the effect.

1. Maria's tire was flat because it had a nail in it.

Correct these sentences.

2. pedro, the owner, walked marsha and me to our table

_____

3. if i give you five nickels, will you give me a quarter

_____

Use context clues to determine the meaning of the bolded words below.

4. When Rachel won the prize she had always wanted, she was **elated**.

_____

5. She was **persistent** and didn't give up trying out for the team.

Thursday 14

Correct these sentences.

1. did allison broke her leg yesterday

_____

2. shelton watched as the zoo keeper feeds the animals

_____

Which word is NOT spelled correctly?

3. odd   redy   magnet   speedy

4. story   handle   gane   fair

Which word does not belong in the group?

5. sandals   socks   gloves   sneakers

Name:

Friday ⬠14

Read the following paragraph and decide if the underlined part has a capitalization error, punctuation error, spelling error, or no mistake. Fill in the circle beside the answer you choose.

<u>australia is the smallest continent</u>. It is the only continent
            1

<u>located entirely inn the</u> southern hemisphere. The <u>kangaroo is the national</u>
     2   **3**

symbol of <u>Australia? Australia's</u> capital is Canberra, located in the
               4

<u>eastern parte of the country.</u>
     5

1. ○ capitalization ○ punctuation ○ spelling ○ no mistake
2. ○ capitalization ○ punctuation ○ spelling ○ no mistake
3. ○ capitalization ○ punctuation ○ spelling ○ no mistake
4. ○ capitalization ○ punctuation ○ spelling ○ no mistake
5. ○ capitalization ○ punctuation ○ spelling ○ no mistake

Answer Key ⬠14

Monday
1. Red, yellow, and blue are primary colors.
2. It was time for dinner. I set the table.
3. gold
4. four
5. closed

Tuesday
1. antonyms
2. antonyms
3. Have you read <u>The Enormous Crocodile</u>, a book by Roald Dahl?
4. I really like to listen to the radio while I jog.
5. noun

Wednesday
1. Maria's (tire was flat) <u>because it had a nail in it.</u>
2. Pedro, the owner, walked Marsha and me to our table.
3. If I give you five nickels, will you give me a quarter?
4. happy, excited, thrilled
5. not giving up, untiring, staying on task

Thursday
1. Did Allison break her leg yesterday?
2. Shelton watched as the zoo keeper fed the animals.
3. redy (ready)
4. gane (gain)
5. gloves

Friday
1. capitalization
2. spelling
3. no mistake
4. punctuation
5. spelling

 Daily Language Review Grade 3 EMC 581

Which word IS spelled correctly?

1. malebox   mailbox   mailbocks   malbox

2. amimal   aminal   animal   annimal

Correct these sentences.

3. did you remember to pack a toothbrush nightgown and bathing suit

4. derrick his favorite subject is art

Complete the following analogy.

5. 7 : number :: G :

Correct these sentences.

1. me and sam want to help mrs james wash her car

2. have you ever been on a airplane

Use context clues to determine the meaning of the bolded words below.

3. On Halloween he will **masquerade** as a ghost using a sheet.

4. He was **ailing** so he stayed home from school and went to the doctor.

Statement, command, question, or exclamation?

5. Have you ever seen the Grand Canyon

Name: _____

Wednesday 15

Is the subject or predicate underlined?

1. Maria and Jason <u>threw a surprise party for their mother</u>. ....

2. <u>The Great Barrier Reef</u> is 1,250 miles long. ....

Correct these sentences.

3. helen keller was learned how to use sign language when she was for

....

....

4. the elephant drawed water in using his trunk he sprayed it on his back

....

....

Which word IS spelled correctly?

5. dangerous   dangerus   dangirus   dangeris

⬠   ⬠   ⬠

Name: _____

Thursday 15

Correct these sentences.

1. doesnt you have to brothers and one sister

....

2. please stand in line for the picture said the teacher

....

Use context clues to determine the meaning of the bolded word below.

3. The book was so **enthralling**, that we wanted to keep on reading.

....

Past, present, or future?

4. The plane landed on time at Dallas Fort Worth Airport. ....

5. Her baggage will be sent to her later.

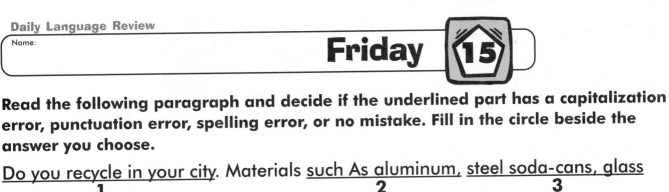
Read the following paragraph and decide if the underlined part has a capitalization error, punctuation error, spelling error, or no mistake. Fill in the circle beside the answer you choose.

<u>Do you recycle in your city</u>. Materials <u>such As aluminum,</u> <u>steel soda-cans, glass</u>
     1   **2**   **3**

containers, and paper can all be recycled. Recycling <u>help's save raw materials that</u>
                                                    4

producers and consumers <u>need to use? It</u> also keeps materials out of landfills and
                              5

helps in the reduction of pollution.

1. ◯ capitalization   ◯ punctuation   ◯ spelling   ◯ no mistake
2. ◯ capitalization   ◯ punctuation   ◯ spelling   ◯ no mistake
3. ◯ capitalization   ◯ punctuation   ◯ spelling   ◯ no mistake
4. ◯ capitalization   ◯ punctuation   ◯ spelling   ◯ no mistake
5. ◯ capitalization   ◯ punctuation   ◯ spelling   ◯ no mistake

Daily Language Review

Answer Key
15

Monday
1. mailbox
2. animal
3. Did you remember to pack a toothbrush, nightgown, and bathing suit?
4. Derrick's favorite subject is art.
5. letter

Tuesday
1. Sam and I want to help Mrs. James wash her car.
2. Have you ever been on an airplane?
3. dress up
4. sick
5. question

Wednesday
1. predicate
2. subject
3. Helen Keller was taught how to use sign language when she was four.
4. The elephant drew water in using his trunk. He sprayed it on his back.
5. dangerous

Thursday
1. Don't you have two brothers and one sister?
2. "Please stand in line for the picture," said the teacher.
3. interesting, fascinating
4. past
5. future

Friday
1. punctuation
2. capitalization
3. no mistake
4. punctuation
5. punctuation

Monday 16

Common or proper noun?

1. San Francisco

2. feather

Correct these sentences.

3. the teacher has brung her chair out to recess she want to read in the fresh air

4. lorie yelled hold that door open for me

Give a synonym for the following word.

5. burglar

Tuesday 16

Correct these sentences.

1. the bunny was fed carrots lettuce and radishes

2. we have studied mars venus and mercury in science

Give a fact about the following topics.

3. Exercise

4. Chicken noodle soup

Use the pair of homophones in one sentence.

5. there, their

Wednesday 16

Complete the analogy.

1. fiction : untrue :: non-fiction : ....

2. Q : capital :: t : ....

Identify the verb in the sentence.

3. He blinked at the bright light.

Correct these sentences.

4. me and you can order a pizza from domino's on friday night

....

....

5. have you read the book sideways stories from wayside school

....

....

Thursday 16

Correct these sentences.

1. how much money do you have left from lunch

....

2. they has a truck a car and a bike in there driveway

....

Which are the singular nouns?

3. baseball   mitt   bats   player   outs

Put these words in alphabetical order.

4. short ship shame shave ....

5. balloon baseball bath bakery ....

Name: _____

Friday 16

Combine the two sentences to make one sentence.

1. Have you read The Chocolate Touch? It's a great book.

   _____

2. The timer went off after five minutes. The egg was cooked.

   _____

3. I have a dalmation. Her name is Lady.

   _____

4. Jordan sits in the front of the class. He needs glasses.

   _____

5. Grandma will call this Sunday. She will call at 6:30 p.m.

   _____

Daily Language Review

Answer Key 16

Monday
1. proper noun
2. common noun
3. The teacher has brought (or brought) her chair out to recess. She wants (or wanted) to read in the fresh air.
4. Lorie yelled, "Hold that door open for me!"
5. crook, thief, robber

Tuesday
1. The bunny was fed carrots, lettuce, and radishes.
2. We have studied Mars, Venus, and Mercury in science.
3. Answers will vary.
4. Answers will vary.
5. Answers will vary.

Wednesday
1. true
2. lower case
3. blinked
4. You and I can order a pizza from Domino's on Friday night.
5. Have you read the book Sideways Stories from Wayside School?

Thursday
1. How much money do you have left from lunch?
2. They have a truck, a car, and a bike in their driveway.
3. baseball, mitt, player
4. shame, shave, ship, short
5. bakery, balloon, baseball, bath

Friday
Sentences will vary. Accept any reasonable sentence construction that contains all the information.

1. Have you read a great book called The Chocolate Touch?
2. The timer went off after five minutes and the egg was cooked.
3. I have a dalmation named Lady.
4. Jordan sits in the front of the class because he needs glasses.
5. Grandma will call at 6:30 p.m. this Sunday.

Correct these sentences.

1. blake thompson played the entire game with a hurt finger

2. he are a great artist exclaimed cheng

Which word would be on the page if the guide words were <u>river</u> and <u>rust</u>?

3. rent   road   right   rival

Use context clues to determine the meaning of the bolded words below.

4. He wrote an **inaccurate** answer for the math problem and had to correct it.

5. The **rubbish** was laying outside and around the trash can, making a big mess.

Synonyms or antonyms?

1. dull, bright

2. bruise, wound

In which part of a friendly letter would this appear?

3. How are you? I am doing very well.

Correct these sentences.

4. hurricane hugo hit charlotte north carolina and caused damage

5. i hope it dont rain saturday

Wednesday (17)

Correct these sentences.

1. you can depend on mother picking you up on time

2. dont forget you're appointment with dr hammersmith on tuesday at 400

Is the underlined word a noun, verb, adjective, or adverb?

3. I pledge allegiance to the <u>flag</u> of the United States of America.

4. The <u>fifty</u> stars on the flag represent the fifty states.

Which is the correct way to divide the word into syllables?

5. co-nver-sation   con-ver-sa-tion   conver-sation

Thursday (17)

A, B, C, or D?

1. What is the correct abbreviation for Friday?
   A. fri.   B. Frid   C. Fri   D. Fri.

2. He _____ see the red light turn green.
   A. didnt   B. did'nt   C. didn't   D. Didn't

Which word IS spelled correctly?

3. shurgar   sugar   shugar   suger

Correct these sentences.

4. dorothy brung the gift to her friends party

5. how did this happen asked mrs barber

Name:

Friday  17

Combine the two sentences to make one sentence.

1. I like vanilla ice cream best. I don't like strawberry.

_____

2. John is afraid of roller coasters. He is afraid of heights.

_____

3. May I borrow a sweater? May I borrow the blue one?

_____

4. Go to bed early. Don't watch too much TV.

_____

5. Our Christmas tree has white lights. The lights blink.

_____

Daily Language Review # Answer Key 17

Monday_____
1. Blake Thompson played the entire game with a hurt finger.
2. "He is a great artist!" exclaimed Cheng.
3. road
4. wrong, incorrect
5. trash, garbage

Tuesday_____
1. antonyms
2. synonyms
3. body
4. Hurricane Hugo hit Charlotte, North Carolina, and caused damage.
5. I hope it doesn't rain Saturday.

Wednesday_____
1. You can depend on Mother picking you up on time.
2. Don't forget your appointment with Dr. Hammersmith on Tuesday at 4:00.
3. noun
4. adjective
5. con-ver-sa-tion

Thursday_____
1. D. Fri.
2. C. didn't
3. sugar
4. Dorothy brought the gift to her friend's party.
5. "How did this happen?" asked Mrs. Barber.

Friday_____
Sentences will vary. Accept any reasonable sentence construction that contains all the information.

1. I like vanilla ice cream best, but I don't like strawberry.
2. John is afraid of roller coasters and heights.
3. May I borrow the blue sweater?
4. Go to bed early, and don't watch too much TV.
5. Our Christmas tree has white blinking lights.

Note: comma placement in sentences 1 and 4 not expected of students at this level.

Monday 18

Correct these sentences.

1. andrew forgot his lunch box at school every day

2. the crocodile has swam across the swamp it seen a fish to eat

Which word is NOT spelled correctly?

3. prey   explain   doller   duty

Past, present, or future?

4. The Smithsons will pay their babysitter $3 an hour.

5. Mrs. McFadden brought cookies for her class.

Tuesday 18

Singular or plural?

1. keys

2. family

Give a common noun for the proper noun.

3. The Boxcar Children

Correct these sentences.

4. my favorite magazine, teen beat, comes on thursdays

5. the power will be out from 600 until 830

Name:

Wednesday 18

Where do the following events probably take place?

1. You can renew your book if you aren't finished reading it, or you can check out a new one.

2. The runner slid into homeplate and was safe!

Correct these sentences.

3. her and me selled lemonade for 50 cents an glass.

4. he dont know what his homework is tonight

Which words have 2 syllables?

5. frozen   latitude   flipper   indent

Name:

Thursday 18

Correct these sentences.

1. mr thompson weared a hat gloves and scarf

2. does you have a pen that I can borrow

Which is the correct way to divide each word into syllables?

3. lo-lli-pop   lol-li-pop   lol-lip-op   lo-llip-op

4. mel-ody   melo-dy   mel-o-dy   me-lo-dy

Sentence or not a sentence?

5. Around the corner.

Name:

Friday ⬠18

Combine the two sentences to make one sentence.

1. Mrs. William's baby is a girl. It is due in April.

2. I have a friend. Her name is Peaches.

3. I got a kitten at the animal shelter. I named her Tacie.

4. Nate is late for a meeting. It started at 4:45.

5. Glenda got her ears pierced. She was in 3rd grade.

Answer Key ⬠18

Monday
1. Andrew forgets his lunch box at school every day.
2. A crocodile swam across the swamp and ate a fish.
3. doller (dollar)
4. future
5. past

Tuesday
1. plural
2. singular
3. book
4. My favorite magazine, Teen Beat, comes on Thursdays.
5. The power will be out from 6:00 until 8:30.

Wednesday
1. library
2. baseball field
3. She and I sold lemonade for 50 cents a glass.
4. He doesn't know what his homework is tonight.
5. frozen, flipper, indent

Thursday
1. Mr. Thompson wore a hat, gloves, and scarf.
2. Do you have a pen that I can borrow?
3. lol-li-pop
4. mel-o-dy
5. not a sentence

Friday
Sentences will vary. Accept any reasonable sentence construction that contains all the information.

1. Mrs. William's baby girl is due in April.
2. I have a friend named Peaches.
3. I got a kitten at the animal shelter and named her Tacie.
4. Nate is late for a 4:45 meeting.
5. Glenda got her ears pierced when she was in 3rd grade.

Name: _____

Monday 19

Correct these sentences.

1. he dont feel good today

_____

2. tom has broke the plant stand again

_____

Underline the cause and circle the effect.

3. I wore a raincoat because it was raining.

Fact or opinion?

4. She needs a haircut badly. _____

5. Africa is a continent. _____

Name: _____

Tuesday 19

A, B, C, or D?

1. He _____ be able to come to the surprise party.
   A. willn't   B. won't   C. wont   D. willnt

Correct these sentences.

2. ben dont have no games to play at his house

_____

3. latisha have went to dr martinez because she aint feeling good

_____

_____

Give the plural of these nouns.

4. party _____

5. family _____

Name: _____

Wednesday 19

Give the pronoun that would go with the underlined noun.

1. <u>Steven</u> has three brothers and two sisters. _____

2. <u>Jane and Thomas</u> will be picked up from school. _____

What is the subject of this sentence?

3. Josh and his dog Ziggy explore the woods together.

   A. Josh   B. Josh and his dog Ziggy   C. explore the woods together

Correct these sentences.

4. we eats our lunch at memorial park

_____

5. mrs talbots class is gonna visit the museum wednesday

_____

_____

Name: _____

Thursday 19

Which words have 3 syllables?

1. earthquake   adjective   buffalo   contraction

Correct these sentences.

2. ill gladly give you a dollar in exchange for your for quarters

_____

_____

3. will you ask the waitress for another fork

_____

Does the underlined word have a prefix or suffix?

4. He <u>disagreed</u> with his friend on the subject. _____

5. Soon it will be time for a <u>restful</u> vacation.

Choose the word that best completes each sentence.

1. We need to find _____ orange sweater for the party.

   a   an   these

2. Her dad is the _____ of all of his brothers.

   shorter   short   shortest

3. Andrew had a _____ time at the birthday party.

   best   well   good

4. The test was hard, but Al thought he'd done _____ .

   best   well   good

5. He is _____ a solo in the play.

   sing   sang   singing

Daily Language Review

Answer Key 19

Monday
1. He doesn't feel well today.
2. Tom has broken the plant stand again.
3. I wore a raincoat because it was raining.
4. opinion
5. fact

Tuesday
1. B. won't
2. Ben doesn't have any games to play at his house.
3. Latisha has gone to Dr. Martinez because she isn't feeling well.
4. parties
5. families

Wednesday
1. He
2. They
3. B. Josh and his dog Ziggy
4. We ate our lunch at Memorial Park.
5. Mrs. Talbot's class is going to visit the museum Wednesday.

Thursday
1. adjective, buffalo, contraction
2. I'll gladly give you a dollar in exchange for your four quarters.
3. Will you ask the waitress for another fork?
4. prefix (dis)
5. suffix (ful)

Friday
1. an
2. shortest
3. good
4. well
5. singing

Name: _____

Monday 20

Use context clues to determine the meaning of the bolded words below.

1. He **pleaded** with his dad to increase his allowance to $2 a week.

_____

2. The dog's **incessant** barking all day long drove the neighborhood crazy.

_____

Which word is NOT spelled correctly?

3. erase   enuf   equipment   everyday

Correct these sentences.

4. the guard fell asleep at 400 and waked up at 630

_____

5. mother asked will you iron these shirts

_____

Daily Language Review

Name: _____

Tuesday 20

Past, present, or future?

1. We are playing Monopoly and winning.

2. He will run home when his grandmother calls him for dinner.

Correct these sentences.

3. travis has two cats a fish and three dogs

_____

4. the parking meter was in front of westwood city mall

_____

Which word IS spelled correctly?

5. revew   reveiw   reveu   review

Wednesday 20

Correct these sentences.

1. the director learned our choir group too patriotic songs

2. the car need to be painted because it is rusty

Is the underlined word a noun, verb, adjective, or adverb?

3. The hummingbird <u>hovered</u> above the plant.

What two words make up each contraction?

4. won't

5. isn't

Thursday 20

Does the following word have a prefix or a suffix?

1. untie

Complete the analogy.

2. Halloween : pumpkin :: Easter :

3. sock : foot :: glove :

Correct these sentences.

4. grandpa fixed oatmeal eggs and juice for breakfast

5. dont forget to pick up you're report card on thursday

Choose the word that best completes each sentence.

1. Will you _____ me to the swimming pool?

   take   taken   took

2. The drill _____ an extension cord.

   need   do need   needs

3. _____ keys are hanging in the front door.

   An   The   A

4. Samuel had _____ eyelash on his cheek.

   an   those   a

5. The _____ book I've ever read is <u>Strider</u>.

   good   better   best

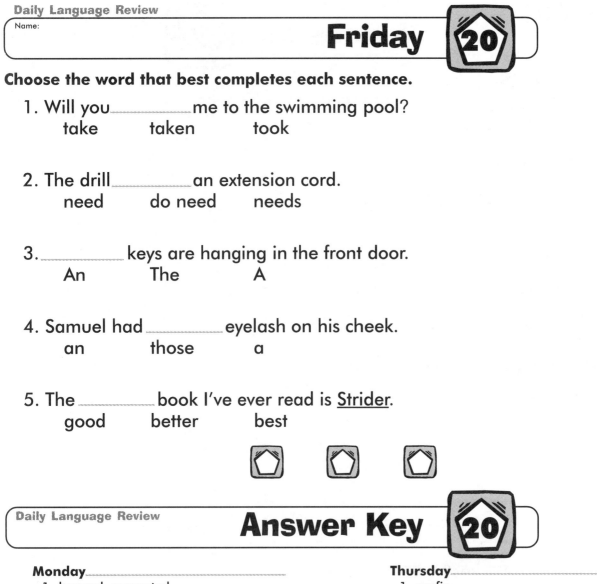

Daily Language Review

Answer Key 20

Monday
1. begged, requested
2. nonstop, constant, continuous
3. enuf (enough)
4. The guard fell asleep at 4:00 and woke up at 6:30.
5. Mother asked, "Will you iron these shirts?"

Tuesday
1. present
2. future
3. Travis has two cats, a fish, and three dogs.
4. The parking meter was in front of Westwood City Mall.
5. review

Wednesday
1. The director taught our choir group two patriotic songs.
2. The car needs to be painted because it is rusty.
3. verb
4. will not
5. is not

Thursday
1. prefix
2. eggs or bunny or cross
3. hand
4. Grandpa fixed oatmeal, eggs, and juice for breakfast.
5. Don't forget to pick up your report card on Thursday.

Friday
1. take
2. needs
3. The
4. an
5. best

Name: _____

Monday 21

Give the past tense of each verb.

1. drive _____

2. listen _____

Exclamation, statement, command, or question?

3. Sharpen all your colored pencils now. _____

Correct these sentences.

4. me and him dont got no homework

_____

5. do you got any work that we can do we want to earn some money

_____

_____

Daily Language Review

Name: _____

Tuesday 21

Which is the correct way to divide the word into syllables?

1. rod-e-o   rode-o   r-od-eo   ro-de-o

Correct these sentences.

2. we watched the lion hunt his prey on a television program

_____

_____

3. does you think this is a good price for notebook paper

_____

Is the subject or predicate underlined?

4. Jason and Tina <u>bought a new house</u>.

5. <u>Taylor Hill</u> has ballet on Mondays and scouts on Wednesdays.

Name: _____

Wednesday 21

Correct these sentences.

1. dad begun to doze off in his chair after dinner

_____

2. my favorite dinosaur is the stegosaurus reported anthony to the class

_____

_____

Put these words in alphabetical order.

3. gasp   garlic   gas   garage _____

4. mirror   minute   misbehave   mink _____

Does the underlined adjective tell how many, which one, or what kind?

5. We still have <u>several</u> students who have not celebrated a birthday this year.

Name: _____

Thursday 21

Give three words that rhyme with each word.

1. time _____   _____

2. day _____   _____   _____

Write one sentence using the homophone pair.

3. for, four

_____

_____

Correct these sentences.

4. jennifer, my best friend, moved to harrisburg pennsylvania

_____

_____

5. on july 4 we will watch the fireworks explode in the sky

Friday 21

Choose the word that best completes each sentence.

1. The plane will be landing within the _____ .
   our   hour   are

2. _____ babysitting for my niece tonight.
   Their   There   They're

3. At the spelling bee she _____ the correct spelling.
   knew   new   knowed

4. Don't forget that your library book is _____ Tuesday.
   do   due   dew

5. The _____ hopped across the street to the other side.
   towed   toed   toad

Answer Key 21

Monday
1. drove
2. listened
3. command
4. He and I don't have any homework.
5. Do you have any work that we can do?
   We want to earn some money.

Tuesday
1. ro-de-o
2. We watched the lion hunt his prey on a television program.
3. Do you think this is a good price for notebook paper?
4. predicate
5. subject

Wednesday
1. Dad began to doze off in his chair after dinner.
2. "My favorite dinosaur is the stegosaurus," reported Anthony to the class.
3. garage, garlic, gas, gasp
4. mink, minute, mirror, misbehave
5. how many

Thursday
1. Answers will vary.
2. Answers will vary.
3. Answers will vary.
4. Jennifer, my best friend, moved to Harrisburg, Pennsylvania.
5. On July 4 we will watch the fireworks explode in the sky.

Friday
1. hour
2. They're
3. knew
4. due
5. toad

Name: _____

Monday (22)

Which word has the same vowel sound as the ea in spread?

1. beneath   weak   tea   bread

Give a synonym for the following words.

2. ill _____

3. enormous _____

Correct these sentences.

4. dr kristensen has telled me to get more exercise

_____

5. we picked up our cat pouncer from the vet at 745

_____

Name: _____

Tuesday (22)

Correct these sentences.

1. luthers favorite book, sarah, plain and tall, is being made into a movie in april

_____

_____

2. them boys was teasing the younger kids at recess

_____

Complete the following analogy.

3. closed : open :: asleep : _____

Give the plural of each noun.

4. class _____

5. box _____

Wednesday 22

Give a proper noun to go with each common noun.

1. restaurant _____

2. teacher _____

Correct these sentences.

3. you may not swim in the pool during adult swim said the lifeguard

_____

_____

4. dads job is not far from our house

_____

Which part of a friendly letter?

5. Dear Seth, _____

Thursday 22

Which words would be on a dictionary page with the guide words <u>mover</u> and <u>muffin</u>?

1. mom   movie   mumble   muddy

Correct these sentences.

2. we heard laughing and clapping in the movie theatre

_____

3. the swamp in lousiana was so dirty that we could not see the alligators

_____

_____

Put these words into alphabetical order.

4. print   press   produce _____

5. alligator   always   allowance _____

Friday 22

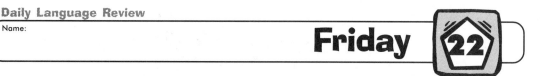

Which reference source would you need to find the following information: dictionary, telephone book, encyclopedia, or thesaurus?

1. what country Juan Peron was president of _____

2. an antonym for "pretty" _____

3. the area codes for your city _____

4. another word for "cry" _____

5. the word origin of the word "spaghetti" _____

Daily Language Review

Answer Key 22

Monday
1. bread
2. sick
3. huge, gigantic, large, massive
4. Dr. Kristensen has told me to get more exercise.
5. We picked up our cat Pouncer from the vet at 7:45.

Tuesday
1. Luther's favorite book, <u>Sarah, Plain and Tall</u>, is being made into a movie in April.
2. Those boys were teasing the younger kids at recess.
3. awake
4. classes
5. boxes

Wednesday
1. Answers will vary.
2. Answers will vary.
3. "You may not swim in the pool during adult swim," said the lifeguard.
4. Dad's job is not far from our house.
5. greeting

Thursday
1. movie, muddy
2. We heard laughing and clapping in the movie theatre.
3. The swamp in Lousiana was so dirty that we could not see the alligators.
4. press, print, produce
5. alligator, allowance, always

Friday
1. encyclopedia
2. thesaurus
3. telephone book
4. thesaurus
5. dictionary

Name:

Monday (23)

Which word does not belong in the group?

1. sea   lake   baseball   ocean   river

2. yellow   round   red   blue   green

Fiction, or nonfiction?

3. Emilio was shrunk to the size of an ant.

Correct these sentences.

4. this roller coaster is fun

5. the irish wear green on st patricks day

Name:

Tuesday (23)

Correct these sentences.

1. sam why wasnt you at the party asked james

2. what time did the accident happen

Use context clues to determine the meaning of the bolded word below.

3. My family **resides** at 1702 Morning Park Lane.

Statement, command, exclamation, or question?

4. Oh, no!

5. My house is near the school.

Name: _____

Wednesday 23

Which word comes LAST in alphabetical order?

1. grade   guide   guest   grin

2. poke   potion   policy   possible

Past, present, or future?

3. Danny and I will be in fourth grade next year. _____

Correct these sentences.

4. can you add subtract and multiply

_____

5. in class today we will read the short story a day at camp

_____

Name: _____

Thursday 23

Correct these sentences.

1. north america is a continent that we are studying

_____

2. he is not gonna get no milk for lunch

_____

If the guide words were <u>exist</u> and <u>explode</u>, which word would be on the page?

3. expire   export   electricity

Synonyms, antonyms, or homophones?

4. dark, bright _____

5. sight, site _____

Friday  23

Which reference source would you need to find the following information: dictionary, telephone book, encyclopedia, or thesaurus?

1. another word for "nice" _____

2. an antonym for "dry" _____

3. how to pronounce "emancipate" _____

4. Where is the museum that is closest to your house? _____

5. How many syllables are in the word "tabulate"? _____

Answer Key 23

Monday
1. baseball
2. round
3. fiction
4. This roller coaster is fun!
5. The Irish wear green on St. Patrick's Day.

Tuesday
1. "Sam, why weren't you at the party?" asked James.
2. What time did the accident happen?
3. lives
4. exclamation
5. statement

Wednesday
1. guide
2. potion
3. future
4. Can you add, subtract, and multiply?
5. In class today we will read the short story "A Day at Camp."

Thursday
1. North America is a continent that we are studying.
2. He is not going to get any milk for lunch.
3. expire
4. antonyms
5. homophones

Friday
1. thesaurus
2. thesaurus
3. dictionary
4. telephone book
5. dictionary

 Daily Language Review Grade 3 EMC 581

Monday (24)

Correct these sentences.

1. do he go to george washington elementary school

   ....

2. dont forget to ask for a receipt

   ....

Give one sentence for each homophone pair.

3. they're, there ....

4. dear, deer ....

Fact or opinion?

5. That book is too long to read in a week. ....

Tuesday (24)

Correct these sentences.

1. we got shampoo soap and a toothbrush at the store

   ....

2. have you memorized you're phone number

   ....

Which one IS a sentence?

3. Karen and Samantha into the store window.

   We study rocks and minerals in science.

A, B, or C?

4. The book report is due ....
   A. October 7 1997   B. October 7, 1997.   C. October, 7, 1997.

5. Did you visit .... last summer?
   A. Denver, colorado   B. denver colorado   C. Denver, Colorado,

Wednesday 24

Complete the analogy.

1. north : south :: east : _____

2. child : children :: party : _____

Is the subject or predicate underlined?

3. <u>I</u> love to listen to the radio in the car. _____

Correct these sentences.

4. he has ate all of the dinner and the dessert

_____

5. my friends robin and lucia has bunk beds in them room

_____

_____

Thursday 24

Where do the following events probably take place?

1. The waitress came to the table to take our order. _____

2. Mrs. Alvarez, the art teacher, passed out glue for our project. _____

Correct these sentences.

3. we memorized the poem called the sneeze for language

_____

_____

4. i dont have no time to go are you going

_____

Which words have 3 syllables?

5. charming   marigold   participate   tremendous

Which reference source would you need to find the following information: dictionary, telephone book, encyclopedia, or thesaurus?

1. the local phone number for the fire department _____

2. what Jim Henson is known for _____

3. the street Kim Li lives on _____

4. the opposite of the word "push" _____

5. a picture of a koala _____

Daily Language Review

Answer Key 24

Monday_____
1. Does he go to George Washington Elementary School?
2. Don't forget to ask for a receipt.
3. Answers will vary.
4. Answers will vary.
5. opinion

Tuesday_____
1. We got shampoo, soap, and a toothbrush at the store.
2. Have you memorized your phone number?
3. We study rocks and minerals in science.
4. B. October 7, 1997.
5. C. Denver, Colorado,

Wednesday_____
1. west
2. parties
3. subject
4. He has eaten all of the dinner and the dessert.
5. My friends Robin and Lucia have bunk beds in their room.

Thursday_____
1. restaurant
2. school
3. We memorized the poem called "The Sneeze" for language.
4. I don't have any (or I have no) time to go. Are you going?
5. marigold, tremendous

Friday_____
1. telephone book
2. encyclopedia
3. telephone book
4. thesaurus
5. encyclopedia

Monday (25)

Correct these sentences.

1. shelly has went to her grandmothers house in nebraska

2. he didnt mean to break the glass it was a accident

Use context clues to determine the meaning of the bolded word below.

3. He tells good jokes and is very **humorous**.

Which word comes first in alphabetical order?

4. planet   pity   plane   plain

5. silver   sign   signal   side

Tuesday (25)

Synonyms, antonyms, or homophones?

1. grow, shrink

2. mystery, puzzle

Correct these sentences.

3. i and jessica have did all the cleaning

4. shannon drunk the punch and eats her sandwich

What is the correct way to divide the word into syllables?

5. in-for-ma-tion   inf-orm-a-tion   in-form-a-tion

Wednesday 25

Which word is NOT spelled correctly?

1. iron   puzle   explain   pear

2. realy   hundred   familiar   diamond

Is the underlined word a noun, verb, adjective, or adverb?

3. The car drove <u>quickly</u> down the narrow alley. _____

Correct these sentences.

4. we always swung in the hammock between the to trees

5. my sisters birthday is march 2 1992 she is younger than i am

Thursday 25

Complete the analogy.

1. December : 12 :: January : _____

2. TV : watch :: radio : _____

Correct these sentences.

3. he dont never do the write page in the math book

4. the read car come toward the building and parked

Identify the adverb in the sentence.

5. I waited patiently for the nurse to call my name.

Name: _____

Friday 25

Read the following paragraph and decide if the underlined part has a capitalization error, punctuation error, spelling error, or no mistake. Fill in the circle beside the answer you choose.

Golf is a <u>popular Sport all over</u> the world. The game is <u>played outdoors over eighteen</u>
1   **2**

holes using a little ball and clubs <u>to hit the ball? The object</u> of the game is to hit the
                                 3

golf ball <u>into a hole 3 1/2 inchs</u> in diameter in as few strokes (hits) as
            4

<u>possible. The winner is the player</u> with the lowest score.
     5

1. ◯ capitalization   ◯ punctuation   ◯ spelling   ◯ no mistake

2. ◯ capitalization   ◯ punctuation   ◯ spelling   ◯ no mistake

3. ◯ capitalization   ◯ punctuation   ◯ spelling   ◯ no mistake

4. ◯ capitalization   ◯ punctuation   ◯ spelling   ◯ no mistake

5. ◯ capitalization   ◯ punctuation   ◯ spelling   ◯ no mistake

Answer Key 25

Monday
1. Shelly has gone to her grandmother's house in Nebraska.
2. He didn't mean to break the glass. It was an accident.
3. witty, funny
4. pity
5. side

Tuesday
1. antonyms
2. synonyms
3. Jessica and I have done all the cleaning.
4. Shannon drank the punch and ate her sandwich.
5. in-for-ma-tion

Wednesday
1. puzle (puzzle)
2. realy (really)
3. adverb
4. We always swing in the hammock between the two trees.
5. My sister's birthday is March 2, 1992. She is younger than I am.

Thursday
1. 1
2. listen
3. He doesn't ever do the right page in the math book.
4. The red car came toward the building and parked.
5. patiently

Friday
1. capitalization
2. no mistake
3. punctuation
4. spelling
5. no mistake

Monday 26

Combine the two sentences to make one sentence.

1. I need to check out a book. The library is closed.

_____

Common or proper noun?

2. Reebok _____

3. Jeffrey Tillston _____

Correct these sentences.

4. wow, that movie at the grand theater was scary

_____

5. at 715 we is gonna have a speaker from phoenix arizona

_____

Tuesday 26

Correct these sentences.

1. we watched the eclipse from are backyard

_____

2. her brother plays basketball soccer and tennis

_____

Write the plural possessive nouns.

3. the room of the girls _____

4. the club of the ladies _____

Combine the two sentences to make one sentence.

5. We rafted down the Ocoee River. The rafting trip lasted six hours.

_____

Name:

Wednesday 26

Which part of a friendly letter?

1. I got a new cat named Topsie on Thursday.

Correct these sentences.

2. if you saw jacob, will you tell him that i need to see him

3. the playground at herman park was flooded during the month of october

Which word does not belong in the group?

4. Africa   Atlantic   Pacific   Indian

5. carrots   lettuce   spoon   tomato

Name:

Thursday 26

Complete the analogy.

1. prefix : beginning :: suffix : _____

2. heart : inside :: skin : _____

Correct these sentences.

3. at 545 the doorbell rang, and we got our pizza from joes pizza palace

4. mrs smothers asked will you be out of town long

Give two words that rhyme with the following word.

5. days _____

Name: _____

Friday 26

Read the following paragraph and decide if the underlined part has a capitalization error, punctuation error, spelling error, or no mistake. Fill in the circle beside the answer you choose.

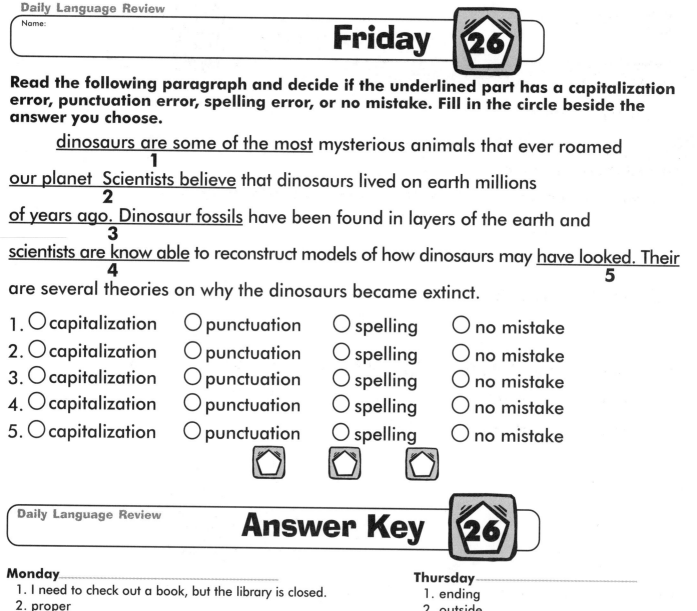

 <u>dinosaurs are some of the most</u> mysterious animals that ever roamed
  1

<u>our planet Scientists believe</u> that dinosaurs lived on earth millions
  2

<u>of years ago. Dinosaur fossils</u> have been found in layers of the earth and
  3

<u>scientists are know able</u> to reconstruct models of how dinosaurs may <u>have looked. Their</u>
  4   **5**

are several theories on why the dinosaurs became extinct.

1. ○ capitalization ○ punctuation ○ spelling ○ no mistake
2. ○ capitalization ○ punctuation ○ spelling ○ no mistake
3. ○ capitalization ○ punctuation ○ spelling ○ no mistake
4. ○ capitalization ○ punctuation ○ spelling ○ no mistake
5. ○ capitalization ○ punctuation ○ spelling ○ no mistake

Answer Key 26

Monday
1. I need to check out a book, but the library is closed.
2. proper
3. proper
4. Wow, that movie at the Grand Theater was scary!
5. At 7:15 we are going to have a speaker from Phoenix, Arizona.

Tuesday
1. We watched the eclipse from our backyard.
2. Her brother plays basketball, soccer, and tennis.
3. girls' room
4. ladies' club
5. We rafted down the Ocoee River for six hours.

Wednesday
1. body
2. If you see Jacob, will you tell him that I need to see him?
3. The playground at Herman Park was flooded during the month of October.
4. Africa
5. spoon

Thursday
1. ending
2. outside
3. At 5:45 the doorbell rang, and we got our pizza from Joe's Pizza Palace.
4. Mrs. Smothers asked, "Will you be out of town long?"
5. Answers will vary.

Friday
1. capitalization
2. punctuation
3. no mistake
4. spelling
5. spelling

Which word has the same sound as the ow in cow?

1. blow   know   frown

Correct these sentences.

2. we is watching carefully to learn how to put the life jacket on

_____

_____

3. the officer said do you know how fast you was going

_____

If the guide words were <u>hike</u> and <u>hit</u>, which words would be on the page?

4. hinge   hijack   high   hire

5. hide   history   hilly   hitch

Does the underlined adjective tell which one, what kind, or how many?

1. I ordered a <u>large</u> pizza to be delivered.

2. There are <u>seven</u> pages missing from my book.

Correct these sentences.

3. he dont like no vegetables fruits or nuts

_____

4. mother asked what time is you gonna be home today

_____

Past, present, or future?

5. My mom is making me a dress for the dance.

Name:

Wednesday 27

Correct these sentences.

1. alicia asked is we gonna carve a pumpkin for halloween

_____

2. he has broke the cords on them fans before it cost ten dollars to fix them

_____

_____

What two words make up the contraction?

3. hadn't _____

4. I'd _____

Which word is NOT spelled correctly?

5. very   really   diferent   supposed

⬠   ⬠   ⬠

Name:

Thursday 27

Singular or plural possessive?

1. tooth's color _____

2. babies' cries _____

Which is the correct spelling for the following word?

3. farthest   farthist   farrthest

Correct these sentences.

4. i got to sisters and won brother in my family

_____

5. me and ed is going to the grocery store to get pasta

_____

Name:

Friday  27

Read the following paragraph and decide if the underlined part has a capitalization error, punctuation error, spelling error, or no mistake. Fill in the circle beside the answer you choose.

Alligators <u>and crocodiles are part of</u> the animal group called <u>crocodilians! Both</u>
             1   **2**

can be dangerous animals. One way <u>to tell A crocodile and an</u> alligator apart is
                                        3

by the <u>shape of they're noses.</u> Alligators have U-shaped noses while
               4

<u>crocodiles noses are</u> more pointed.
  5

1. ◯ capitalization   ◯ punctuation   ◯ spelling   ◯ no mistake
2. ◯ capitalization   ◯ punctuation   ◯ spelling   ◯ no mistake
3. ◯ capitalization   ◯ punctuation   ◯ spelling   ◯ no mistake
4. ◯ capitalization   ◯ punctuation   ◯ spelling   ◯ no mistake
5. ◯ capitalization   ◯ punctuation   ◯ spelling   ◯ no mistake

---

Daily Language Review

Answer Key 27

Monday
1. frown
2. We are watching carefully to learn how to put the life jacket on.
3. The officer said, "Do you know how fast you were going?"
4. hinge, hire
5. history, hilly

Tuesday
1. what kind
2. how many
3. He doesn't like any vegetables, fruits, or nuts.
4. Mother asked, "What time are you going to be home today?"
5. present

Wednesday
1. Alicia asked, "Are we going to carve a pumpkin for Halloween?"
2. He has broken the cord on those fans before. It cost ten dollars to fix them.
3. had not
4. I had, I would
5. diferent (different)

Thursday
1. singular possessive
2. plural possessive
3. farthest
4. I have two sisters and one brother in my family.
5. Ed and I are going to the grocery store to get pasta.

Friday
1. no mistake
2. punctuation
3. capitalization
4. spelling
5. punctuation

Name: _____

Monday (28)

Correct these sentences.

1. what instrument does you play

_____

2. helen rided a horse in the parade on sunday

_____

Give a common noun for the proper noun.

3. Texas _____

4. Africa _____

Write the plural form of the noun.

5. puppy _____

Name: _____

Tuesday (28)

Which word is spelled correctly?

1. punkin   pumkin   pumpkin   pumpckin

2. baskitball   basketball   basketbal   bascketball

Give an opinion about the following:

3. Pizza Hut pizza

_____

Correct these sentences.

4. me and him have a book report that is do tuesday

_____

5. yesterday dad run in the marathon

_____

Which is the correct way to divide each word into syllables?

1. al-li-ga-tor   all-i-ga-tor   al-lig-a-tor

2. alph-a-bet   al-pha-bet   al-phab-et

Correct these sentences.

3. will you gimme another peace of paper

4. saturday we is gonna go to dinner and to a movie

Common or proper noun?

5. Bugs Bunny

Correct these sentences.

1. turn them lights on please

2. last friday we took a family picture at mark smith studio

Give a fact about the following topic.

3. Saturday

Which words rhyme?

4. shoe   toe   glue   flew

5. pancake   remake   true   quake

Name:

Friday 28

Combine the two sentences to make one sentence.

1. The quarterback threw the ball. The receiver dropped it.

2. Juan can recite the alphabet backwards. I can do it to also.

3. Poinsettias are pretty plants. They are red.

4. The battery on the radio went dead. We need a new one.

5. Her family is visiting from Athens, Georgia. I met them last week.

Daily Language Review

Answer Key 28

Monday
1. What instrument do you play?
2. Helen rode a horse in the parade on Sunday.
3. state
4. continent
5. puppies

Tuesday
1. pumpkin
2. basketball
3. Answers will vary.
4. He and I have a book report that is due Tuesday.
5. Yesterday Dad ran in the marathon.

Wednesday
1. al-li-ga-tor
2. al-pha-bet
3. Will you give me another piece of paper?
4. Saturday we are going to dinner and to a movie.
5. proper noun

Thursday
1. Turn those lights on please.
2. Last Friday we took a family picture at Mark Smith Studio.
3. Answers will vary.
4. shoe, glue, flew
5. pancake, remake, quake

Friday
Do not hold children responsible for commas in compound sentences unless this skill has been formally taught.
1. The quarterback threw the ball, but the receiver dropped it.
2. Juan and I can recite the alphabet backwards.
3. Poinsettias are pretty, red plants.
4. The battery on the radio went dead, so we need a new one.
5. Last week I met her family who are visiting from Athens, Georgia.

Name:

Monday 29

Correct these sentences.

1. grandmothers making me an blew dress

2. would you like sum cinnamon toast

Which word does not belong in the group?

3. huge   enormous   tiny   giant   large

4. December   Thursday   June   April   October

Use context clues to determine the meaning of the bolded word below.

5. The lion tamer's shirt was **tattered** after the lion tried to scratch him.

Name:

Tuesday 29

What contraction would the two words make?

1. I would

2. we will

Correct these sentences.

3. the dog chewed my knew shoes

4. did you get your ears pierced at bertrams fine jewelry

What is the subject in the following sentence?

5. The hammer is broken.

Name: _____

Wednesday 29

Correct these sentences.

1. last week i talk so much my throat hurt

_____

2. i got a doctors appointment tuesday at 745

_____

What do the following words have in common?

3. Mars   Earth   Jupiter   Neptune _____

4. ten   fifty   seventy   thirty _____

Underline the cause and circle the effect.

5. He ate too many candy bars so he got fat.

Name: _____

Thursday 29

What two words make up the contraction?

1. wouldn't _____   _____

2. I'll _____   _____

Correct these sentences.

3. who wrote the book wayside school is falling down

_____

4. please set the alarm clock to woke up at 600 am

_____

Combine the sentences to make one sentence.

5. I went to New Orleans. I visited my grandfather.

Name: _____

Friday  29

Combine the two sentences to make one sentence.

1. I've heard that song on the radio. I don't remember who sings it.

_____

2. Reagan's dad is my dentist. He is very nice.

_____

3. We walk the dog after dinner. We walk a mile and a half.

_____

4. Hayden is a gymnast. She is very flexible.

_____

5. I asked for a Sega for Christmas. I didn't get the Sega.

_____

Answer Key 29

Monday
1. Grandmother's making me a blue dress.
2. Would you like some cinnamon toast?
3. tiny
4. Thursday
5. ripped, torn

Tuesday
1. I'd
2. we'll
3. The dog chewed my new shoes.
4. Did you get your ears pierced at Bertram's Fine Jewelry?
5. The hammer

Wednesday
1. Last week I talked so much my throat hurt.
2. I have a doctor's appointment Tuesday at 7:45.
3. planets
4. numbers (multiples of 10)
5. He ate too many candy bars so he got fat.

Thursday
1. would not
2. I will, I shall
3. Who wrote the book Wayside School is Falling Down?
4. Please set the alarm clock to wake up at 6:00 a.m. (or A.M.)
5. I went to New Orleans and visited my grandfather.

Friday
Sentences will vary. Accept any reasonable sentence construction that contains all the information. Don't hold children responsible for commas in compound sentences unless this skill has been formally taught.

1. I've heard that song on the radio, but I don't remember who sings it.
2. Reagan's dad is my dentist, and he is very nice.
3. We walk the dog a mile and a half after dinner.
4. Hayden is a very flexible gymnast.
5. I asked for a Sega for Christmas, but I didn't get it.

Monday 30

Replace each underlined pronoun with a proper noun.

1. <u>He</u> doesn't understand his math homework. _____

2. Jordan will give <u>her</u> the pages to read. _____

Does the following word have a prefix or suffix?

3. easily _____

Correct these sentences.

4. were only allowed to watch one our of television on saturdays

_____

5. did you vote for ben lily or armond for class president

_____

Tuesday 30

Correct these sentences.

1. my friend alicia drives to fast

_____

2. dr barger run past the nurse he gave a patient a note

_____

Which part of a friendly letter?

3. Your friend, _____

4. 1922 Beverly Drive _____

Does the underlined adjective tell which one, what kind, or how many?

5. Will you taste <u>this</u> sauce and tell me if it has too much salt?

Name: _____

Wednesday 30

Give two words that rhyme with the following words.

1. tall _____   _____

2. town _____   _____

Correct these sentences.

3. bruce he is gonna be a snake in the play

_____

4. did you read the short story called sleeping ugly

_____

How many syllables in the word?

5. neighbor _____

Name: _____

Thursday 30

Correct these sentences.

1. im gonna be a model when i grow up

_____

2. lester, my brother, will be six years old on friday

_____

Give an opinion about the following topic.

3. aliens

_____

What do the following words have in common?

4. ball   globe   circle   ring _____

5. soccer   football   hockey   tennis _____

Combine the two sentences to make one sentence.

1. The ball came straight to him. He caught it.

2. Our team wears blue and white. They are losing now.

3. Rebecca plays tennis on Thursdays. She is very good.

4. We got a new computer. It has a CD ROM.

5. The plant has turned brown. It needs water.

Daily Language Review

Answer Key 30

Monday
1. Answers will vary.
2. Answers will vary.
3. suffix (ly)
4. We're only allowed to watch one hour of television on Saturdays.
5. Did you vote for Ben, Lily, or Armond for class president?

Tuesday
1. My friend Alicia drives too fast.
2. Dr. Barger ran past the nurse. He gave a patient a note.
3. closing
4. heading
5. which one

Wednesday
1. Answers will vary.
2. Answers will vary.
3. Bruce is going to be a snake in the play.
4. Did you read the short story called "Sleeping Ugly"?
5. 2

Thursday
1. I'm going to be a model when I grow up.
2. Lester, my brother, will be six years old on Friday.
3. Answers will vary.
4. they are all round
5. they are all sports

Friday
Sentences will vary. Accept any reasonable sentence construction that contains all the information. Don't hold children responsible for commas in compound sentences unless this skill has been formally taught.

1. The ball came straight to him, and he caught it.
2. Our team, in the blue and white, is losing now.
3. Rebecca plays tennis on Thursdays, and she is very good.
4. We got a new computer with a CD ROM.
5. The plant has turned brown because it needs water.

Monday (31)

Divide each word into syllables.

1. rotate _____

2. huddle _____

Correct these sentences.

3. the falcon caught its prey while flying it was a pigeon

_____

4. we have forgot to water the plants i hope they arent dead

_____

_____

Underline the cause and circle the effect.

5. The fire was extinguished because the firemen sprayed it with water.

Tuesday (31)

Correct these sentences.

1. in gym we jump rope play volleyball and run

_____

2. our class went to the houston zoo on a field trip last april

_____

_____

Which word is NOT spelled correctly?

3. principal   hippopotamus   illegal   minite

Where does each quotation probably take place?

4. "Fasten your seatbelts." _____

5. "The sign says not to feed the animals." _____

Name: _____

Wednesday 31

Sentence or not a sentence?

1. Karen has a beautiful voice. _____

Correct these sentences.

2. dont be late for your piano lessons said mother

_____

3. our team wears read shirts for field day last month

_____

What is the prefix or suffix in the words?

4. valuable _____

5. hibernating _____

Name: _____

Thursday 31

Correct these sentences.

1. what are you going to do after school today asked sandy

_____

2. ive got to tell you what our assignment is in social studies

_____

Complete the analogies.

3. Valentine's Day : hearts :: St. Patrick's Day : _____

4. day : awake :: night : _____

How many syllables in the word?

5. publication _____

Name: _____

Friday 31

Choose the word that best completes each sentence.

1. Colin and _____ are in the same class at school.

     me   I   us

2. The point goes to Karleigh and _____ .

     me   I   us

3. They did a very _____ job on the book report.

     better   good   well

4. Casper, Wyoming, _____ a beautiful city.

     is   am   are

5. The plane _____ landed on time.

     was   have   has

Daily Language Review

Answer Key 31

Monday
1. ro-tate
2. hud-dle
3. The falcon caught its prey while flying. It was a pigeon.
4. We (have forgotten or forgot) to water the plants. I hope they aren't dead.
5. The fire was extinguished because the firemen sprayed it with water.

Tuesday
1. In gym we jump rope, play volleyball, and run.
2. Our class went to the Houston Zoo on a field trip last April.
3. minite (minute)
4. car, truck, airplane
5. at the zoo or park

Wednesday
1. sentence
2. "Don't be late for your piano lessons," said Mother.
3. Our team wore red shirts for field day last month.
4. -able (suffix)
5. -ing (suffix)

Thursday
1. "What are you going to do after school today?" asked Sandy.
2. I've got to tell you what our assignment is in social studies.
3. shamrocks, leprechauns
4. asleep
5. 4 (four)

Friday
1. I
2. me
3. good
4. is
5. has

Name:

Monday 32

Correct these sentences.

1. how many times have you saw the movie the lion king

2. susan she has gave me her lunch money every day

Is the underlined word a noun, verb, adjective, or adverb?

3. The <u>television</u> was turned to channel 7.

4. Her mother lives <u>nearby</u> in Center, Texas.

What time of day does the following probably take place?

5. We turned off all the lights, locked the doors, and got our pajamas on.

Name:

Tuesday 32

Sentence or not a sentence?

1. Randy and Steven sang the song together.

Correct these sentences.

2. janet asked did you tried to call me last night

3. i forget to get my math science and language books

Which word is NOT spelled correctly?

4. ladies   boxs   churches   puppies

5. participate   obvious   mashine   label

Wednesday 32

Give the comparative and superlative adjectives.

1. small _____

2. good _____

Past, present, or future?

3. We went to the book fair this morning. _____

Correct these sentences.

4. does you know the author of the book the enormous egg

_____

5. i am not gonna get on no airplane shouted andrew

_____

Thursday 32

Correct these sentences.

1. the weather man said that a cold wind will come threw on tuesday

_____

_____

2. i hope you brung a jacket for the field trip

_____

What is the root or base word in each word?

3. suddenly _____

4. misspell _____

Which IS the correct spelling?

5. brekfast   breakfist   breakfast

Friday  32

Choose the word that best completes each sentence.

1. _____ you ever been horseback riding?

    Is   Have   Has

2. We _____ known each other for six years.

    is   have   has

3. _____ mother plays bridge with my mother.

    Johns   Him's   John's

4. Trey _____ always wanted to be a dentist.

    is   have   has

5. They _____ doing a great job decorating the house.

    are   was   is

Daily Language Review

Answer Key 32

Monday
1. How many times have you seen the movie "The Lion King"?
2. Susan has given me her lunch money every day.
3. noun
4. adverb
5. night, bedtime

Tuesday
1. sentence
2. Janet asked, "Did you try to call me last night?"
3. I forgot to get my math, science, and language books.
4. boxs (boxes)
5. mashine (machine)

Wednesday
1. smaller, smallest
2. better, best
3. past
4. Do you know the author of the book The Enormous Egg?
5. "I am not going to get on an airplane!" shouted Andrew.

Thursday
1. The weather man said that a cold wind will come through on Tuesday.
2. I hope you brought a jacket for the field trip.
3. sudden
4. spell
5. breakfast

Friday
1. Have
2. have
3. John's
4. has
5. are

Name: _____

Monday 33

How many syllables in each word?

1. ornament _____

2. laboratory _____

Give one sentence with the homophone pair.

3. nose, knows

_____

Correct these sentences.

4. is carmen in you're class this year again asked sheldon

_____

5. brandon he has missed for days of school during the month of december

_____

_____

Daily Language Review

Name: _____

Tuesday 33

Correct these sentences.

1. my mother is gonna make brownies for my birthday on august 13 1997

_____

_____

2. our neighbor mrs thomas has a brown dog named midnight

_____

Fact or opinion?

3. My potato has too much butter.

4. It took us thirty minutes to drive to the beach. _____

Sentence or not a sentence?

5. This weekend. _____

Name: _____

Wednesday (33)

Underline the cause and circle the effect.

1. He ate all of the Halloween candy and got a stomachache.

Replace each underlined pronoun with a proper noun.

2. <u>You and I</u> are going to have a great lunch! ·····················

3. Danny called <u>him</u> on Saturday afternoon. ·····················

Correct these sentences.

4. paul and rebecca is gonna by the new house on 1334 oak street

·····················

·····················

5. peaches, my cat, got declawed on friday

·····················

Name: _____

Thursday (33)

Correct these sentences.

1. danielle said i am waiting for a phone call from my boss

·····················

·····················

2. i won't never touch those toys again

·····················

Where does each quotation probably take place?

3. "Are we going to get to milk the cows and ride a horse?"

·····················

4. "The dressing room is right here. Let me know if you need another size."

·····················

Identify the prefix or suffix in the word.

5. helpful ·····················

Choose the word that best completes each sentence.

1. Rachel _____ a blue and white car.
   drived   drives   drive

2. She _____ to wear silver jewelry.
   likes   like   is liking

3. Eugene _____ to go to school in Oklahoma.
   want   are wanting   has wanted

4. They _____ skiing in Taos, New Mexico.
   are   is   have

5. Will you decide who is going with _____?
   us   they   I

Daily Language Review

Answer Key (33)

Monday
1. 3
2. 5
3. Answers will vary.
4. "Is Carmen in your class this year again?" asked Sheldon.
5. Brandon has missed four days of school during the month of December.

Tuesday
1. My mother is going to make brownies for my birthday on August 13, 1997.
2. Our neighbor Mrs. Thomas has a brown dog named Midnight.
3. opinion
4. fact
5. not a sentence

Wednesday
1. He ate all of the Halloween candy and got a stomachache.
2. Answers will vary.
3. Answers will vary.
4. Paul and Rebecca are going to buy the new house on 1334 Oak Street.
5. Peaches, my cat, got declawed on Friday.

Thursday
1. Danielle said, "I am waiting for a phone call from my boss."
2. I won't ever touch those toys again!
3. a farm
4. a clothing store, a fitting room
5. -ful (suffix)

Friday
1. drives
2. likes
3. has wanted
4. are
5. us

Name:

Monday 34

Correct these sentences.

1. will you gimme for sheets of paper on wednesday

2. our teacher has learned us how to do multiplication

Give an antonym for each word.

3. high

4. plain

Does the underlined adjective tell which one, what kind, or how many?

5. Her <u>older</u> brother plays basketball on Thursdays.

Name:

Tuesday 34

Divide each word into syllables.

1. farmer

2. headquarters

Is the underlined word a noun, verb, adjective, or adverb?

3. Her sister <u>flew</u> in from Nebraska yesterday at 4:35.

Correct these sentences.

4. the united states of america has three branches of government

5. have you studied synonyms antonyms and homophones yet this year

Wednesday 34

Give the pronouns in each sentence.

1. He will give her piano lessons on Tuesdays at 7:30. ....

2. Will you give him the correct pages to read? ....

Correct these sentences.

3. does you like to ride in dads car or moms

4. we will vote for president of the united states in november

Give one sentence with the homophone pair.

5. sew, so

Thursday 34

Correct these sentences.

1. did you know that elections are always the first tuesday after the first monday in november

2. i am gonna invite edward robert and kaitlin to my party on saturday its at the skating rink

Past, present, or future?

3. She is reading <u>Sarah, Plain and Tall</u> to our class. ....

Write the comparative and superlative adjectives.

4. short

5. bad

Friday  34

Which reference source would you need to find the following information: dictionary, almanac, telephone book, encyclopedia, or thesaurus?

1. another word for "guest"   _____

2. how the -ough sounds in the word "tough"   _____

3. which state is known for making the most toothpicks   _____

4. how many miles between Miami, Florida, and Dallas, Texas _____

5. the years that Marie Curie lived   _____

Answer Key 34

Monday _____
1. Will you give me four sheets of paper on Wednesday?
2. Our teacher has taught us how to do multiplication.
3. low
4. fancy, decorated, mountain
5. which one

Tuesday _____
1. far-mer
2. head-quar-ters
3. verb
4. The United States of America has three branches of government.
5. Have you studied synonyms, antonyms, and homophones yet this year?

Wednesday _____
1. he, her
2. you, him
3. Do you like to ride in Dad's car or Mom's?
4. We will vote for President of the United States in November.
5. Answers will vary.

Thursday _____
1. Did you know that elections are always the first Tuesday after the first Monday in November?
2. I am going to invite Edward, Robert, and Kaitlin to my party on Saturday. It's at the skating rink.
3. present
4. shorter, shortest
5. worse, worst

Friday _____
1. thesaurus
2. dictionary
3. encyclopedia, almanac
4. almanac
5. encyclopedia, almanac

Monday 35

Which word is NOT spelled correctly?

1. ponyes   babies   daisies   countries

2. ghost   guest   ghastly   guid

Correct these sentences.

3. first i am washing my car i am gonna wash karens next

_____

4. her long thick brown hair takes ours to dry

_____

Give a proper noun for the common noun.

5. country _____

Tuesday 35

Does the following word have a prefix or suffix?

1. ironing _____

Give a synonym for each word.

2. smaller _____

3. wrong_____

Correct these sentences.

4. he will have a meeting this thursday at 345

_____

5. ouch that really hurt yelled paul to his brother

_____

Wednesday 35

Give three words that rhyme with each word.

1. across _____ _____

2. sneeze _____ _____

Correct these sentences.

3. we didnt never see who stole the cookies from the cookie jar

_____

4. does you like to play the game monopoly or the game sorry

_____

Divide the word into syllables.

5. informal _____

Thursday 35

Sentence or not a sentence?

1. A cup of cold water is so refreshing on a hot day. _____

2. Into the oven. _____

Correct these sentences.

3. for field day i entered the three-legged race the hoop shoot and the peanut run

_____

_____

4. is they coming to see the play called the clown who ran away

_____

_____

Complete the analogy.

5. January : _____ :: August : summer

Which reference source would you need to find the following information: dictionary, almanac, telephone book, encyclopedia, or thesaurus?

1. a synonym for the word "find"

2. the difference between frogs and toads

3. the address for Pete's Deli

4. how many definitions the word "run" has

5. the names of all of the colleges
   and universities in the United States

Daily Language Review

Answer Key **35**

Monday
1. ponyes (ponies)
2. guid (guide)
3. First I am washing my car. I am going to wash Karen's next.
4. Her long, thick, brown hair takes hours to dry.
5. Answers will vary.

Tuesday
1. suffix (-ing)
2. Answers will vary.
3. Answers will vary.
4. He will have a meeting this Thursday at 3:45.
5. "Ouch! That really hurt!" yelled Paul to his brother.
            OR
   "Ouch, that really hurt!" yelled Paul to his brother.

Wednesday
1. Answers will vary.
2. Answers will vary.
3. We didn't see who stole the cookies from the cookie jar.
4. Do you like to play the game Monopoly or the game Sorry?
5. in-for-mal

Thursday
1. sentence
2. not a sentence
3. For field day I entered the three-legged race, the hoop shoot, and the peanut run.
4. Are they coming to see the play called The Clown Who Ran Away?
5. winter

Friday
1. thesaurus
2. encyclopedia
3. telephone book
4. dictionary
5. almanac

Monday 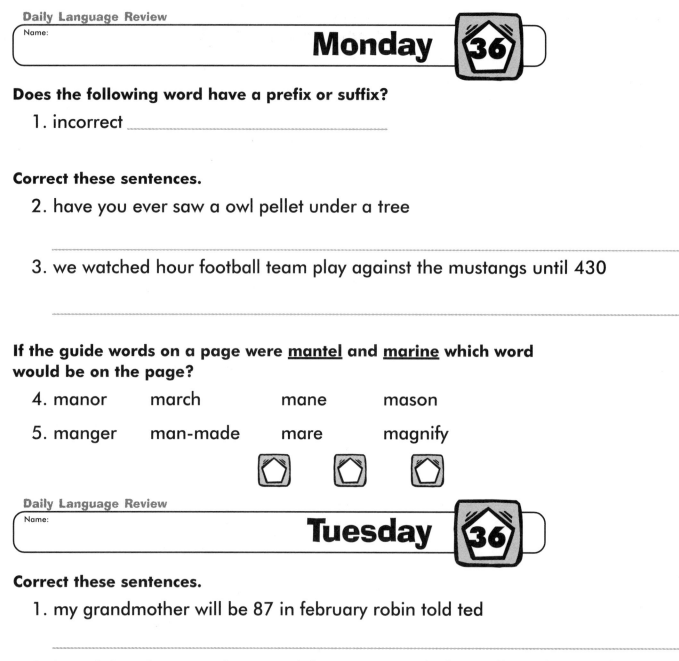 36

Does the following word have a prefix or suffix?

1. incorrect _____

Correct these sentences.

2. have you ever saw a owl pellet under a tree

_____

3. we watched hour football team play against the mustangs until 430

_____

If the guide words on a page were <u>mantel</u> and <u>marine</u> which word would be on the page?

4. manor   march   mane   mason

5. manger   man-made   mare   magnify

Tuesday 36

Correct these sentences.

1. my grandmother will be 87 in february robin told ted

_____

2. it took her three weeks to peel the paper patch the walls and paint them

_____

What do these words have in common?

3. kangaroo   pogo sticks   hopscotch

4. grass   chameleon   avocado

Where does the quotation probably take place?

5. "Please change the channel to the news for a minute."

Name: _____

Wednesday (36)

Give an antonym for each word.

1. strong ....

2. grown-up ....

Give one sentence with the homophone pair.

3. deer, dear

....

Correct these sentences.

4. trent asked what time does the lunch start should i bring anything

....

....

5. we will have cake when dinner is finished mother said to hayden

....

....

Name: _____

Thursday (36)

Correct these sentences.

1. next year im gonna be in forth grade remarked anna

....

2. i hopes you will be in my class joana said to alyssa

....

Past, present, or future?

3. I brought my teacher an apple on the last day of school. ....

4. She will be teaching third grade again next year. ....

Divide the word into syllables.

5. trustworthy _____

Friday  36

Which reference source would you need to find the following information: dictionary, almanac, telephone book, encyclopedia, or thesaurus?

1. the name of a store that fixes televisions _____

2. the opposite of the word "solid" _____

3. the current population of Northern Ireland _____

4. information to write a report on Neptune _____

5. the phone number for South Park Mall _____

Daily Language Review

Answer Key 36

Monday
1. prefix (in)
2. Have you ever seen an owl pellet under a tree?
3. We watched our football team play against the Mustangs until 4:30.
4. march
5. mare

Tuesday
1. "My grandmother will be 87 in February," Robin told Ted.
2. It took her three weeks to peel the paper, patch the walls, and paint them.
3. they jump
4. they are green
5. at home watching TV

Wednesday
1. Answers will vary.
2. Answers will vary.
3. Answers will vary.
4. Trent asked, "What time does the lunch start? Should I bring anything?"
5. "We will have cake when dinner is finished," Mother said to Hayden.

Thursday
1. "Next year I'm going to be in fourth grade," remarked Anna.
2. "I hope you will be in my class," Joana said to Alyssa.
3. past
4. future
5. trust-wor-thy

Friday
1. telephone book
2. thesaurus
3. almanac
4. almanac, encyclopedia
5. telephone book